This series offers the concerned reader basic guidelines
and *practical* applications of religion for today's world.
Although decidedly Christian in focus and emphasis,
the series embraces all denominations and modes of
Bible-based belief relevant to our lives today. All volumes
in the Steeple series are originals, freshly written to
provide a fresh perspective on current—and yet timeless—
human dilemmas. This is a series for our times.

Among the books in the series:

Woman in Despair: A Christian Guide to Self-Repair
Elizabeth Rice Handford

How to Read the Bible
James Fischer

Bible Solutions to Problems of Daily Living
James W. Steele

A Book of Devotions for Today's Woman
Frances Carroll

Temptation: How Christians Can Deal with It
Frances Carroll

*With God on Your Side: A Guide to Finding
Self-Worth through Total Faith*
Douglas Manning

*Help in Ages Past, Hope for Years to Come:
Daily Devotions from the Old Testament*
Robert L. Cate

*A Daily Key for Today's Christians:
365 Key Texts of the New Testament*
William E. Bowles

*Walking in the Garden:
Inner Peace from the Flowers of God*
Paula Connor

Help in Ages Past, Hope for Years to Come

Daily Devotions from the Old Testament

Robert L. Cate

A SPECTRUM BOOK

Prentice-Hall, Inc.,
Englewood Cliffs, New Jersey 07632

Library of Congress Cataloging in Publication Data

Cate, Robert L.
  Help in ages past, hope for years to come.

  (Steeple books)
  "A Spectrum Book."
  Includes index.
    1. Bible. O.T.—Devotional literature.   I. Bible.
  O.T. English. Revised Standard. Selections. 1983.
  II. Title.   III. Series.
  BS1151.5.C37 1983   242'.5   83-3324
  ISBN 0-13-387449-4
  ISBN 0-13-387431-1 (pbk.)

ISBN 0-13-387449-4

ISBN 0-13-387431-1 {PBK.}

Unless otherwise indicated, Scripture quotations are from the Revised
Standard Version of the Bible, copyrighted 1946, 1952, © 1971, 1973.

Editorial/production supervision by Eric Newman
Cover design by Hal Siegel
Manufacturing buyers: Christine Johnston and Edward J. Ellis

This book is available at a special discount when ordered in
bulk quantities. Contact Prentice-Hall, Inc., General
Publishing Division, Special Sales, Englewood Cliffs, N.J. 07632.

Prentice-Hall International, Inc., *London*
Prentice-Hall of Australia Pty. Limited, *Sydney*
Prentice-Hall Canada Inc., *Toronto*
Prentice-Hall of India Private Limited, *New Delhi*
Prentice-Hall of Japan, Inc., *Tokyo*
Prentice-Hall of Southeast Asia Pte. Ltd., *Singapore*
Whitehall Books Limited, *Wellington, New Zealand*
Editora Prentice-Hall do Brasil Ltda., *Rio de Janeiro*

To my students,
who have expressed a need for
and offered encouragement in
the development of these devotionals

Contents

Preface

This book is intended to help you develop, maintain, and enrich your personal devotional life with God. We all struggle with this and usually need all the help we can get.

If you have had trouble getting started on a plan of daily devotions, this book will help you. It has a systematic arrangement designed to guide you in covering a broad spectrum of devotional thoughts related to the whole of life's experiences. Not selected at random, but with intent, these devotions will enrich your spiritual life. Furthermore, if one selection or another is more appropriate at any given moment, you can skip from section to section. However, I suggest that you deal fully with all the devotions in a particular section before moving on to another.

Furthermore, if you have had difficulty breaking away from the same old, familiar passages in your devotional life, this book will force you to explore the riches of God's Word in some unfamiliar passages. Many of us confine our devotional reading of the Bible to the very familiar or sometimes only to the New Testament. These devotions, although written from a Christian standpoint, are all taken from the Old Testament. You will hear God speak in a new and fresh way from verses that may be less familiar to you.

If you are a mature Christian and a church leader, you have probably spent most of your time in Bible study looking for what God is saying to those with whom you work and to whom you minister. It is quite easy to so listen for His Word to others that we never hear His Word to us. These devotions are aimed at helping you listen to what God is saying to *you*. This will further enrich your life and help you grow in Christ.

Finally, if you are a student, you may be spending so much time on the academic study of the Bible or of religion that you are not listening for God's Word *to you*. I am seeking to help you allow God to confront you personally through His Word. I am a professor of the Old Testament. I have done the academic study of these passages before preparing these devotionals. But academics should not shut God out. Sometimes, we allow the academic study of the Bible to take the place of listening to God. This book will help you change this.

God has riches to share with you. He has given them to the saints of the ages. He will enrich your life through these same truths. Join me in a pilgrimage through the first half of His Word, listening to what He has to say to you in the Old Testament.

chapter one

The Ear That Listens

HEARING THE TESTIMONY OF OTHERS

> We have heard with our ears, O God,
> our fathers have told us,
> what deeds thou didst perform in their days,
> in the days of old.
>
> *PSALM 44:1*

God expects His people to have a listening ear. You and I must learn to listen *for* His voice. But having heard His voice, we must learn to listen *to* His voice. Both of these things must be done long before we try to tell others what He has said. That should be obvious. It should be, but it frequently isn't. Far too often we are guilty of speaking about God from our ignorance.

For the child of God, however, merely listening to the voice of God is not enough. We must also listen to the voices of those around us. In most conversations, you and I are so busy thinking about what we are going to say next that we fail to hear what people are saying to us. The listening ear becomes the characteristic of a caring, concerned, compassionate person. It tells others that we think they are important. And they are important. They are important to God. They should be important to us. The first way by which we can show their importance to us is by listening to what they have to say.

There is a tendency for those of us who have been deeply involved in Christianity for a long time to make two assumptions about listening to others. First, we assume that we have heard everything. We begin to believe that no one has anything new to say to us. That is false. Even though experiences which different people have may be similar, the uniqueness of each individual makes each experience unique. Our second assumption is just as false, and this is that our own experience with God is normative. This error makes us pass judgment on the spiritual experience of others before we really listen to them. How sad.

The folly here rests in the fact that we tend to develop an air of spiritual superiority. This comes from an attitude which implies "I know it all and I have experienced it all. There is nothing new that you can say to me about life or about God." I cannot think of an attitude more foreign to the Spirit of Christ or to the message of the Bible.

Consider again the words of the psalmist in our text. His prime confidence rested not only in his own experience but in his hearing from others what God had done with them. He was not judging their experience by his own, but he was judging his experience by theirs. His listening ear had opened up new vistas of truth and revelation. If you and I are to grow in our knowledge and understanding of God, we must become people who listen to the testimony of others. Their experience with God may provide a new key to help us understand our own.

It is that simple.

But it is also that profound.

O Thou who hast spoken through the saints of old as well as ultimately through Thine own Son, speak to us now by the presence and power of Thy Spirit through the words of others. Help us to make our ears listen to their testimony and experience. In Jesus' name we pray. Amen.

RECOGNIZING THE VOICE OF GOD

> And the Lord came and stood forth,
> calling as at other times, "Samuel! Samuel!"
> And Samuel said, "Speak, for thy servant hears."
>
> *1 SAMUEL 3:10*

How can we recognize the voice of God? Young Samuel grew up in the temple of Shiloh. He slept in the sanctuary, to be available should any need arise. On this particular night his sleep was disturbed on three occasions by a voice calling him, rousing him from his sleep. Each time he ran to Eli, the priest, thinking that he had called. Finally, Eli suggested that Samuel make the response that is our text: "Speak, for thy servant hears." (A more literal translation is: "Speak, for thy servant is listening.")

At first glance, you and I might find the experience of Samuel quite foreign to anything with which we are familiar. But a second thought helps us to identify with it. In all honesty, we must admit that we have a great deal of difficulty in identifying the voice of God from all the other voices and sounds we hear.

If we are going to be serious about our servanthood, we are going to have to be serious in trying to filter out all other voices we hear. We must identify the voice of God from among them.

God speaks to us through the experiences of life. We may hear His voice in the voice of friends or family. We may hear Him through the sounds of nature or through the whimper of a hungry child. We may hear Him from the pages of a book or through a voice on the television. If we believe that He can and does speak to us in such diverse manners, then it becomes our responsibility to develop the spiritual sensitivity, the personal awareness, and our divine-human relationship, so that we are tuned in to God's voice when He does speak.

But there is another side to that process. We must also be able to recognize those times when God is not speaking. Amos heard God speak through the lion's roar. Elijah heard Him in the still, small voice. Habakkuk, on the other hand, agonized over the other issue, saying, "O Lord, how long shall I cry for help, and thou wilt not hear?" (Hab. 1:2). Since he did not hear God, he assumed God did not hear him. We must be able to decide when the voice we hear is our own inner desires and not the voice of God. We must be just as able to decide when someone else speaks as if from God, but God is not in it. One of the key issues in the Old Testament is how to determine who is a false prophet. That issue is no less important now. We need to be able to recognize the voice of God.

Recognizing God's voice is no less difficult for us than it was for the saints of yesteryear. If I had an infallible system for identifying the voice of God from all the other voices that I hear, I would gladly share it. In all honesty, I do not have such a system. But one thing I do know: The first step to hearing the voice of God is to have a listening ear. You and I as God's servants must be listening for the voice of God. I must do my best to be attentive. I must be *trying* to hear. Somehow, through all the static and the distractions, God's voice will get through.

Almighty God, Thou who hast spoken to us in the days past, speak to us now through the presence of Thy Holy Spirit. May He indwell our lives and guide our minds, to the end that we may hear and obey Thy voice. Through Jesus Christ our Lord we pray, in Whom Thou has spoken to us most fully. Amen.

HEARING THE TEACHER

> Come, O sons, listen to me,
> I will teach you the fear of the Lord.
> *PSALM 34:11*

One of the most difficult things you and I have to do in our spiritual growth is to learn to listen to those who are teaching us how to follow God. This is not so difficult at the beginning of our spiritual pilgrimage. When we are babes in Christ, we readily acknowledge that almost anyone can teach us spiritual truths. But as the years pass and we begin to think we are growing spiritually mature, we fall victims of self-confidence and pride.

We are usually aware that there are those who are more spiritually mature than we. We are quite willing to listen to such persons and to learn from them. But there are others who also teach us. From them we also learn, if we have the will to listen. These are those who, consciously or unconsciously, intentionally or accidentally, are helping to guide us in the paths of following God. Furthermore, while they are teaching us, we should also be teaching them. We are all fellow pilgrims in our search for God.

It is not hard to accept the fact (self-centered as we are) that we can teach others in their spiritual pilgrimage. It becomes significantly harder to accept the fact that they can teach us as well. It is difficult to believe that spiritual peers can teach us anything. Those who are in the same lifeboat with us in our struggle for spiritual survival have as much or more to teach us as we have to teach them. We must learn to listen to our companions.

But, if it is hard to learn to listen to the spiritual teaching of our peers—and it is—the hardest thing of all is learning to listen to those whom we consider less spiritually mature. It is not so difficult to listen to the advice of those who have gone *before* us, and it is far more difficult to listen to the advice of those who are struggling up the slopes of life *with* us, but it is almost impossible to listen to those who are struggling far *behind* us. Yet, we must do so.

It is one of the strange things about spiritual growth that we can all help one another. As a pastor, I have learned much from my congregation about the ways of following and serving God. From the kindergarten children I have learned about openness, trust, and love. As a seminary professor, I have seldom taught a class in which my students have not taught me something about God's Word and will or about commitment and dedication.

You see, it matters not where we are on the spiritual or intellectual ladders of growth, anyone who is a fellow pilgrim may become our teacher along the way. There are those amazing moments when, by the grace of God, our lives interact. At that moment, we may discover that we have become both teacher and pupil. This is all-important, for we must be aware that we are also teachers of God's people. This responsibility can never be ignored. But even more importantly, we must also be aware that we are called on to listen to and learn from our fellow pilgrims. We must listen for the voice of God as He speaks to us through our teachers, whoever they may be.

Help us, O Lord, to know that we aren't spiritual experts so much as spiritual blunderers saved from our folly by Your grace, for Christ's sake we pray. Amen.

IDENTIFYING THE VOICE OF GOD

And he said, "Go forth, and stand upon the mount before the Lord." And Behold, the Lord passed by, and a great and strong wind rent the mountains, and broke in pieces the rock before the Lord, but the Lord was not in the wind; and after the wind an earthquake, but the lord was not in the earthquake; and after the earthquake a fire, but the Lord was not in the fire; and after the fire a still small voice.

1 KINGS 19:11-12

Somehow, it appears that most of us wish to be like Paul, struck down on the road to Damascus, when we hear the voice of God. Or at least, we wish to be like Amos, who said that the voice of God was like a lion's roar. We would like God to speak to us in such spectacular ways that our attention is captured and thus we will never have any question as to whether or not what we heard was the voice of God. It isn't always like that at all.

More often we can identify with Elijah, who was so attuned

to the voice of God on Carmel that all the shouting of the prophets of Baal never drowned out the voice of God. He knew that God had spoken in the fire of Carmel. Then Jezebel threatened his life. Suddenly, her threat was so loud that he couldn't hear God any longer. So he turned away from the place of his ministry and ran for his life.

When he arrived at Horeb (Sinai), Elijah was so impressed with his own importance in the kingdom of God that he expected some great, thundering revelation. He expected God to speak spectacularly. This was so true that the prophet almost missed the "still, small voice." Literally, God spoke to him in "a voice of silent quietness." The message from God was so unspectacular, he almost missed it.

This can happen to you and me. We expect the voice of God to come to us in some kind of striking revelation. More often than not, God speaks to us in a "voice of silent quietness," and we are likely to miss it if we aren't really tuned in to Him.

Two men strolled down the sidewalk of a busy street in a major city. In the background were all the noises of the typical urban setting. One turned to the other and said, "You tell me that you frequently hear God speak to you. Well, I've never heard God speak." The second man did not respond, but reached into his pocket, withdrew a coin, and casually flipped it off to the side. There, in the midst of all the noises of the city traffic, the coin clinked on the sidewalk. Suddenly the first man stopped, saying, "What was that?" Without even slowing down, the second responded, "We hear what we listen for!" And so we do!

It is wonderful when God speaks in the thunder's roll or the lion's roar. But it is no less wonderful when He speaks in the still, small voice. It is just harder to hear out of the midst of all those voices that clamor for our attention. We must be listening for the voice of God so that we hear Him, regardless of how He speaks. We must be able to identify His voice. Before we can become obedient servants, we must first be listening servants. There is no other way.

Teach us to turn our attention on Thee, O Lord, that we may hear Thy voice whenever it calls for our attention. May we never fail to hear thee because we listen for the wrong things. This we pray in Jesus' name and for His sake. Amen.

LISTENING FOR THE VOICE OF GOD

> Morning by morning he wakens,
> he wakens my ear
> to hear as those who are taught.
> The Lord God has opened my ear,
> and I was not rebellious,
> I turned not backward.
>
> *ISAIAH 50:4b-5*

In the discipline of listening for the voice of God, in the process of seeking to "tune in" to the voice of God while "tuning out" all those other voices that clamor for our attention, one thing which we should never forget is that even the process of listening to the voice of God is a gift of God's grace. It is God who makes it possible for us to listen to Him in the first place. In our text, God's servant acknowledges the fact that God "wakens [his] ear."

Before we ever begin to attune our minds and lives to the voice of God, He begins to tune us in. The initiative in our hearing God's voice always rests with God. In other words, He starts to communicate on our frequency. God comes to us with His message for us. He is not just "out there" somewhere talking, hoping that we will turn Him on. He comes, speaking specifically to you and to me, saying to us precisely what we need to hear.

The Servant of God was clearly aware that God was turning him into a disciple. That relationship still holds for us as well, whenever God speaks. He is the Teacher. You and I are the pupils, "those who are taught." It is our task and responsibility to be open to the voice of God. More than this, it is our opportunity to receive the voice of God. And what an opportunity it is!

Yet, as we pause and wonder at the opportunity God gives us in hearing the voice of the Creator, who has become our Redeemer, of the Sovereign Lord of the universe, who has become the Suffering Savior of mankind, we must also face the tragedy of our failure to listen to Him. All too often we cannot say with the servant in our text, "I was not rebellious, I turned not backward." For you and I are rebellious at the voice of God. We do turn away backward.

The voice of God comes, teaching us an uncomfortable truth—we are neither lovely nor lovable. It is that which we do not wish to hear. Yet, the voice of God also comes with the comfort of His love.

Furthermore, God's voice points us to the hurting humanity in His world and to the injustices of our social orders. We cannot really listen to the voice of God and be content any longer with things as they are. God comes to us proclaiming the truth as it is for people as they are. But He also comes offering the vision of what can be in place of the reality of what is.

By His grace, He speaks to us.

By His grace, He lets us listen.

By His grace, He allows us to respond.

By His grace, He leaves us free to rebel—or to obey. The choice is always ours.

We thank Thee, Lord, for coming to us while we were yet sinners, awakening us in our sins, calling us to Thyself, cleansing us from our sin, and sending us back into Thy world to minister in Thy name. Help us listen to Thy voice and to respond in obedient love. Amen.

SHUTTING OUT THE VOICE OF GOD

> How can you say, "We are wise,
> and the law of the Lord is with us"?
> But, behold, the false pen of the scribes
> has made it into a lie.
> The wise men shall be put to shame,
> they shall be dismayed and taken;
> lo, they have rejected the word of the Lord
> and what wisdom is in them?
>
> *JEREMIAH 8:8-9*

There is a tendency in the human heart we need to be aware of. It is present in me, I know. I suspect that it is also present in you. This is the tendency to reject any message from God that we do not wish to hear. We accomplish this in a number of ways.

We reject God's voice through self-confident pride. When we become so confident that we have God's revelation in full and that we no longer need to listen to the voice of His Holy Spirit, we have rejected His message. When we become so proud of the fact that we have the Bible and possess it in all the latest translations, yet never seek to obey its insistent demands, we have rejected His message. We may possess the Bible, but it has never possessed us.

We also reject God's voice by pretending that we do not understand it. We may not understand it all, but we are responsible for obeying what we *do* understand. A theological smoke screen is no excuse for failing to obey what we have clearly heard.

Furthermore, we reject God's voice by focusing so much on the problems of His Word that we ignore its demands. There are problems. No one can deny that. But there are sublime teachings as well, where there are no problems at all except our lack of obedience.

We may also allow the weaknesses of our fellow Christians to become a stumbling block to obedience. However, these weaknesses pale into insignificance before the sublime figure of the Lord Jesus. Neither the problems of His word nor those of His people should be allowed to cause us to fail to hear and heed His voice.

Finally, we reject God's voice by becoming too wrapped up in it. That sounds quite strange. Yet it is quite true. We may analyze, categorize, and synthesize theological systems about God and His message. We can become so involved with all the minutiae of doctrine that we never respond to God's voice at all. We have become quite adept at debating about uncomfortable truths while ignoring God's insistent demands. The voice of God always demands a response.

No one is wise who has sought to establish his or her life upon the rejection of the voice of God. No one is wise, no matter how effectively we may debate the meaning of God's Word, if we are not busy obeying Him in effective, relevant, compassionate service. If I have not heard the voice of God, it may be because I have refused to hear it. If you have not heard His voice, it may be for the same reason. In either case, there is no wisdom in us. Thus, professing ourselves to be wise, we have become fools. Let us never shut out the voice of God.

Keep us, Father, from becoming so wise in our own eyes that we become fools. Help us, rather, to listen to Thy voice, to ponder what we do not understand, and to obey what we clearly know. This we pray in the name of Him who showed us fully what it means to obey Thy voice. Amen.

chapter two

The Eye That Sees

SEEING THROUGH THE MISTS OF DOUBT

At the end of all the conflicts, troubles, and agonies of Job, he finally said to God,

> "I had heard of thee by the hearing of the ear,
> but now my eye sees thee;
> therefore I despise myself,
> and repent in dust and ashes."
>
> *JOB 42:5-6*

For faith to be real, there must come a time when it stops being something that has been passed on to you, and becomes instead the fruit of your own experience. Faith that has been passed on to you by parents, teachers, or pastors may be adequate for life as long as no great crises come along to threaten it. But faith that is second hand is seldom adequate for dealing with the deepest issues of life. When real life crises come, you must have something more than "hand-me-down" faith.

There is a time in spiritual growth for asking, "What do I believe about this?" or "What should I believe about that?" But we must move beyond this in our spiritual pilgrimage to where we can say, "This is my faith, fashioned in the furnace of my experience with God."

Admittedly, it sounds quite arrogant to stand before the world saying, "Here I stand. This is my faith. Upon it I am building my life." At the same time, however, that arrogance passes into honest self-confidence when the beliefs on which you are standing are not something others have told you, but spring from your own experience with God and His Word.

A life built on God's Word and on personal experience with God will have a few absolutely solid convictions on which to stand, come hell or high water. If these convictions become too numerous, they cease being fundamental, and our lives become shaky.

It is a good spiritual discipline to periodically (at least once a year) ask youself, "What are the basic items of faith for which I am willing to die and by which I am willing to live?" These should not simply include opinions loosely held or ideas for which you can amass a long list of reasonable arguments. Rather, these must be things of ultimate commitments.

These ultimate commitments should be relatively stable. If they change too much from time to time, they were not very good convictions in the first place. But if they never change at all, then you are not growing. The way you phrase them, or arrange them, or emphasize them will change, or you have probably become a dead head.

Job discovered that what he had received by hearing about God was not really adequate for meeting the crises of life. It was not until he had personally experienced God that his faith became adequate. This does not mean that what he had received was wholly wrong. It only means that no faith is adequate until it has been certified or adapted by our own experience with God. When we finally see God as He is, then we ultimately see ourselves as we are. This is where faith begins—and ends.

Give us, O Lord, eyes to see Thy Spirit at work in our lives, that our faith may be strong in Thee. In Jesus' name we pray. Amen.

When the servant of Elisha saw the armies of Syria surrounding his city, he was overwhelmed by a sense of utter helplessness. This placed him in complete despair.

> Then Elisha prayed, and said, "O Lord, I pray thee, open his eyes that he may see." So the Lord opened the eyes of the young man, and he saw; and behold, the mountain was full of horses and chariots of fire round about Elisha.
>
> *2 KINGS 6:17*

Most of us who seek to follow the way of Christ in this world some time or another come to the place where we have an experience similar to that of Elisha's servant. Our lives have been going along quite smoothly, with a deep sense of satisfaction, regular evidence of God's blessings, and occasional high moments of spiritual victory. Or, at least, this is the way life appears to us. Suddenly, a major crisis either threatens or actually comes, and we find ourselves swamped by a sense of utter helplessness and complete despair.

At such times, our usual reaction is to ask in wondering fear, "Where has God gone?" Or at least we query, "Why has God done this to me?" The problem, as usual, does not rest with God, but with us. It is our vision that has failed us.

The world is so much with us and we are so much a part of it, that when crises come we lose any spiritual insights we might have attained. We claim ourselves to be realistic, and so we are. There is nothing wrong with that. At least, there is nothing wrong with that until we begin allowing our "realism" to limit our understanding of God.

When Jesus was confronted by a hungry multitude, the realistic disciples saw only a lad with his lunch, but Jesus was able to meet their needs with those resources. It was not Jesus' lack of power but their lack of vision that was the problem. This is still true today. A major part of spiritual growth is the development of spiritual vision. We need to learn to see not only the cold, hard facts, but the amazing resources of God.

Many people saw the rising smoke of the incense in the Temple in the year of King Uzziah's death. But Isaiah had a vision of the exalted Lord, and he responded with a life of devoted service. Many shepherds heard the lions' roar in the Judean wilderness during the days of Jeroboam II of Israel. But Amos heard the voice of God and devoted his life in an attempt to help his people escape the coming judgment. Many people had marriages break up in the last days of the kingdom of Israel. But Hosea heard God speak to him through his heartbreak and shared with his people the message of God's love that would overcome their infidelities.

The constant message of the Bible is that God's people must learn to see through the eyes of faith. Only those who see the invisible can do the impossible. When our gaze is attracted by things that are too near to us, our vision becomes limited. Our prayer must be that God will improve our vision, so that we may see His handiwork. His love and His power are not limited. It is simply that we frequently fail to see them because we do not look.

Merciful Father, allow us to see beyond the experiences of time to the things of eternity. Help us to see not only the tragedy, but the triumph as well. This we pray in Jesus' name. Amen.

SEEING GOD'S GREAT ACTS

And the Egyptians shall know that I am the Lord, when I stretch forth my hand upon Egypt and bring out the people of Israel from among them. . . . By this you shall know that I am the Lord: behold, I will strike the water that is in the Nile with the rod that is in my hand, and it shall be turned to blood.

EXODUS 7:5, 12

In the Old Testament, the verb *to know* does not merely refer to something we have learned intellectually; it really refers to something we have learned by experience. Furthermore, it also refers to the most intimate kinds of personal experience. God's warning to Pharaoh and His admonition to Moses and Israel in our text can only be fully understood when we first understand what God means by "know."

The primary purpose of the so-called plagues of Egypt was neither to punish Egypt nor even to deliver Israel from slavery. God could have done either or both of these things with much greater simplicity. Instead, God bluntly announced that the purpose of the plagues was to allow both Egypt and Israel to experience His sovereign Lordship over all the earth. In order for them to fully grasp this fact, it was required that all the people involved should have their eyes opened to see God's great acts.

From the standpoint of either the Egyptians or the Hebrews, many of the events that occurred could have been explained as an unusual and catastrophic experience of natural events. Frogs, locusts, hail, storm, disease, all of these may have been abnormal, but they probably would not have been considered supernatural. On the other hand, with Moses announcing in advance that the plagues were coming and telling when they were leaving, it became more than a mere set of coincidences. Most important of all, each of the plagues was actually a contest between the gods of Egypt and the God of Israel. In each contest, the God of Israel won!

As Moses clearly pointed out the fact that the plagues were sent by Israel's God, both Israel and Egypt had their eyes focused on the great acts of God. They saw His sovereign power over both natural and historical forces.

It is at this point that we come face to face with God's definition of "to know." We need to turn our attention upon the great acts of God, seeing them (and therefore experiencing them) as His sovereign acts over the universe. The eyes of faith are able to see the hand of God at work in the world. Unbelieving eyes are seldom convinced by miracles. But faith is confirmed by those same events in the eyes of those who already have experienced

God. Miracles do not produce faith. On the other hand, faith sees the miracles of God in the world.

God's great acts are intended to help us experience His sovereign Lordship. We are all spiritually blind until God comes to help us see. It is easy to see the hand of God at work in the world when you have experienced God at work in your life. It is God's intent that we have the spiritual vision to see His work in our world. He works that we may "know" that He is the Lord and that we may experience His loving power.

O Thou God of powerful love, open our eyes that we may see Thy mighty acts. Give us the sight to see Thy sovereign love. We thank Thee for what we have experienced of Thee in the past, and beg that we may have new experiences in the future. This we pray in Jesus' name. Amen.

SEEING WHEN SIGHT FAILS

For I know that my Redeemer lives,
and at last he will stand upon the earth;
and after my skin has been thus destroyed,
then from my flesh I shall see God,
whom I shall see on my side,
and my eyes shall behold, and not another.
My heart faints within me!

JOB 19:25-27

Catastrophe comes in many forms. It visits us as tragedy, worry, grief, pain, and death. The Biblical image of a person who faced such tragedy is Job. Stripped of property, bereft of family, and deprived of health, his faith was tested to the extreme.

In his weaker moments, he lashed out at God, friends, and even his wife. But we do him an injustice if this is all we see in his experience. In his moments of greater faith, he ascends to spiritual heights that beckon us to follow. Our text portrays one of these mountaintops.

The grief of Job's painful present frequently blinded him to any other realities. Then, there would suddenly burst upon his inner sight a vision that lifted him above his present to the brighter vision of a better future. We, like Job, need to develop the faith to help us see when sight fails.

We need first of all to see that we have not been left alone. We may lose our perception of God's presence and love, but we are never abandoned. He is always there. Job could say with his renewed spiritual vision that his Redeemer lived. This is still so for us today.

The concept of "Redeemer" in the Old Testament is of one who is nearest of kin. Job was aware that God had assumed that relationship to him. As such, God would take care of all Job's needs and obligations. He still does this for us. If we can see that God has become our nearest kinsman, taking upon Himself all obligations for us, then we can rise above any present crisis.

But we must also see that not only has God not deserted us, but that He draws nearer to us in the midst of our catastrophes. It is one thing to say that God is always there. It is quite another to be aware that He draws especially close in our times of greatest need. When we need Him most, He is most present.

Perhaps Job's greatest awareness of God's presence and power showed forth in his awareness that he would personally experience God's sustaining grace and love. Job did not have to rely on someone else's encouraging word. He was going to experience God's love personally. Now *that is hope*! Out of the midst of whatever crisis and tragedy comes in life—and they do come—we will personally experience God's loving presence. This is our hope. It was sufficient for Job. It is sufficient for us.

When tragedy comes, God comes. And God is always stronger and more powerful than any tragedy. The message of Job is that

God is with us. In moments of deepest gloom, we can see the brightest hope of His presence. That was sufficient for Job. It is sufficent for us. "I know that my Redeemer lives." That is enough.

When griefs overwhelm us, O Lord, help us to know Thy redeeming, sustaining presence. May we have the insight to see and experience Thy presence in the depths of our heartbreak. This we pray in the name of Him who came to fully show that Thou art with us, Jesus our Lord. Amen.

SEEING WHAT PEOPLE REFUSE TO SEE

And Gideon said to him, "Pray, sir, if the Lord is with us, why then has all this befallen us? And where are all his wonderful deeds which our fathers recounted to us, saying, 'Did not the Lord bring us up from Egypt?'"

JUDGES 6:13

A common question from those who have trouble believing the Biblical message is, "Where are all the miracles?" We get the impression as we read the Bible that every time God's people were in difficulties, he performed some great miracle of deliverance. This reasoning leads to the assumption that we should have just as many miracles today as those ancient peoples did, if God is a God of miracles.

The basic problem with this kind of thinking is that it is based on a false assumption. We assume that miracles in Biblical times were both frequent and easily recognized. It comes, then, as quite a shock to us when we confront the question Gideon addressed to God. Simply paraphrased, Gideon was asking, "Where are all the miracles that we have heard about?" Gideon had been told that God was a God of miracles. In the midst of his difficulties, he wanted to see some of those miracles. He even questioned whether or not God cared for his people. At least to Gideon, miracles were neither frequent nor easily seen.

We could go afield with all sorts of theological discussions concerning the whole concept of miracles. For our purpose here, however, it would be a digression from the basic issue. The real issue raised by our text can be phrased in one of two ways. We could ask the question: Are miracles absent just because they are not perceived? The question could also be phrased: Does God not care about us just because we don't see evidence of His power in miraculous acts?

Put thus bluntly, it is obvious that both questions deserve a negative answer. God does care about us, even when we do not see evidence of His power in miraculous acts. Further, just because we do not see or perceive His miraculous acts does not mean that they do not occur. The blind cannot see a rose, but roses do exist. The child taking his first tottering steps may not perceive the sustaining power of his nearby parent, but that does not indicate that it is absent.

Gideon and his people did not perceive the loving care of God because their problems were too close to them. Yet God still loved and cared for them. The presence of trouble does not mean the absence of God. Gideon wanted to see a miracle; God offered His presence instead. Gideon wanted proof; God expected faith instead. Trust based upon certainty demands no faith.

Contemporary Christianity speaks a great deal of the need for faith in God. This is a proper emphasis. Unfortunately, we all too often act as if we cannot believe unless there is certain proof. When there is such proof, no faith is required. God asks us to have eyes to see what others refuse to see. This requires faith. Wonderfully, faith is something that all can have. It is also something that all must have. We must not look so hard for miracles that we fail to see God. For it is only as we see God that we can begin to see His miracles.

O Thou who spoke the worlds into existence, speak to our hearts, that we may begin to really exist in Thy loving presence. Help us to trust Thee day by day that we may live with Thee throughout eternity. Give us eyes to see Thy presence in all of life. This we pray in the name of Thy Son, our Lord. Amen.

SEEING IN PROPER PERSPECTIVE

When I look at thy heavens, the work of thy fingers,
the moon and the stars which thou has established;
what is man that thou art mindful of him,
and the son of man that thou dost care for him?

PSALM 8:3-4

Driving in parts of the southwestern United States, I occasionally have the experience of seeing, rising out of the desert, a mountain that appears to be quite close. Even though I have been tempted to leave my car and walk over to the mountain, I resist the temptation, for experience has shown me that the mountain may be as far as fifty miles away. When the mountain is seen against the flat desert wastes, my perception gets completely distorted, so that I do not properly evaluate my relation to the mountain.

We have all seen the moon rise on the eastern horizon. While it is still on the horizon, the moon appears to be quite large. Later, after it has gotten farther up in the sky, the moon appears to be much smaller. Yet, when we measure the actual diameter of the moon as we view it, we discover that it is exactly the same, whether seen against the horizon or high in the sky. Again, it is our perception of the moon that changes, not the moon itself.

The same thing is true of spiritual matters. When you and I begin to consider the vastness of this universe, we are awed by its immensity. Considering the size of the earth, with its multiplied millions of people, and then comparing that with our solar system, with our galaxy, and then with the numbers of galaxies beyond, we are staggered by the universe of which we are a part. Against such a background, one individual appears to be utterly insignificant.

It was precisely that which staggered the imagination of the psalmist. Given the vastness and complexity of our universe, he cried out, "What is man?" Yet, that did not drive the psalmist to despair. For he knew with all of his being that God was mindful of His people, each and every one of them. The vastness of the universe did not cause the psalmist to lose his belief that God cared for him. Instead, it caused him to pause in even greater awe that the Creator and Sustainer of the universe really did care for His people.

Perhaps the most important thing for you and me to do is to get things in their proper perspective. God did create this universe. He is still in control of it. But even more important, He cares for you. He cares for me.

I do not know why God is "mindful" of us. But I know beyond a doubt that He is. I also know that there is nothing in either you or me to attract God's love. We are unlovely and unlovable. But He loves us just the same. This God takes time out from running the universe to care for you and me. Now that is news! That is good news, indeed!

You and I may let things get out of perspective. God does not. The world is not more important to Him than an individual. Whenever I begin feeling down and out, or unimportant, I remind myself that God cares for me. Further, when I get down on someone else, I remind myself that God cares for that person as well. I dare not let anything else distract me from that. God loves you and me.

We do not understand, O Lord, how Thou canst keep us in mind in the midst of all the things that demand Thy concern. But we re-

joice in the fact that Thou dost. Help us never to forget that Thy people are of prime importance to Thee. This we pray through Jesus Christ, our Lord. Amen.

chapter three
The Voice That Speaks

HEARING GOD'S VOICE IN NATURE

> The heavens are telling the glory of God;
> and the firmament proclaims his handiwork.
> Day to day pours forth speech,
> and night to night declares knowledge.
> There is no speech, nor are there words;
> their voice is not heard;
> yet their voice goes out through all the earth,
> and their words to the end of the world.
>
> *PSALM 19:1-4*

When we stop to ponder the world of nature around us, there are many things that move us deeply. The sunset, the fresh blooming flower, the dewdrop on the spider's web, the searing flash of lightning—these all communicate orderliness, beauty, change, and power. But whatever it is that impresses us, that causes us to pause and wonder for a moment, there is always something beyond the wonder that tugs at us deep within. There is an awareness of a deeper reality that attracts us, deeper than that which is important in the world.

It is that deeper awareness of which the psalmist speaks. In the world of nature, God speaks to the hearts of all men everywhere. There is no real voice. Neither are there actual words. But the world around us speaks to us of God in a very real, though almost indefinable way.

To the people of the Bible, there was never any doubt but

that God was in the world of nature. At the same time, neither was there any doubt that there was a quantitative and qualitative difference between the way in which God was in the world and the way in which God was "in Christ." Yet that does not negate the fact that God is in the world.

From that concept, it was just a step for Biblical people to realize that God speaks through the world of nature. From the scientist in the laboratory to the child who wonders at the expanding horizons of his or her world, all become aware that God is speaking in the world. When we are aware that God is speaking, it becomes possible for us to hear Him.

Ancient man saw the lightning flash and thought that God had thrown a thunderbolt from heaven. Modern man, realizing that lightning is caused by electrons rubbing off of turbulent molecules, sometimes fails to realize that electrons and molecules have not done away with God. Someone made the molecules the way they are. Our explanations have merely expanded the horizons of our knowledge. But God still speaks to us from those expanded arenas of experience.

It is important for us to begin to listen to the voice that speaks through the world of nature. We should learn to listen not merely to the sounds of man's accomplishments, but to the voice of God who has made all this possible. When God speaks, we should listen. Let us resolve to listen to His voice in the world around us.

God of creative power and wisdom, help us to listen to Thy voice in the world around us. May we not become so engrossed with our own wisdom and accomplishments that we fail to hear Thee speak through Thy creation. We are grateful that Thou hast given us the world in which to live and to love Thee. Through Jesus' name we pray. Amen.

HEARING GOD'S VOICE IN HIS WORD

The law of the Lord is perfect, reviving the soul;
the testimony of the Lord is sure, making wise the simple;
the precepts of the Lord are right, rejoicing the heart;
the commandment of the Lord is pure, enlightening the eyes;
the fear of the Lord is clean, enduring for ever;
the ordinances of the Lord are true, and righteous altogether.

PSALM 19:7-9

One of the greatest gifts God has provided for us is His Word. To the ancient Hebrew, the written Word of God was a precious treasure. It was honored, preserved, studied, memorized, and obeyed.

Modern people sometimes find the whole idea of God giving law to His people to be both restrictive and frustrating. To the Hebrew, this idea was wonderful. It showed them that God cared for them and was concerned with the quality of their life. It also made life livable.

It should do the same for us. Children quickly learn that no game is playable without rules. Football would become impossible if a touchdown counted six points for one team and ten points for the other. If a first down were earned after ten yards gained by one team, but after twenty yards for the other team, the game would be nonsensical. Furthermore, if no one knew where the goal line was except the referee, the whole experience would become one of utter frustration.

If this is true of a game, it is even more true of life. The rules of life are set forth in His Word so that we can know what it is that makes life not only livable, but worth living. The Word that God has given us helps us to know how to live. If that were all it did, it would be wonderful. But it does much more than that.

God's Word also tells us who He is. In that written self-revelation, God has given to us a record of His actions so that we can begin to know His nature, His character, and His purposes. However, unless we study His Word, we shall never really understand the God which the Bible reveals. Many so-called atheists have not rejected the God of the Bible, but they have devised a mere caricature of Him. Furthermore, one of Satan's greatest tricks is to get us so hung up on some of the problem passages of the Bible that we fail to comprehend the simple portrait of God it reveals.

Now I would never claim that all there is to know about God can be found within the pages of a sacred Scripture, but it certainly offers us the best, clearest place to begin. It is through the words of Scripture that we come face to face with God.

If you and I are ever going to really know God, we must begin with His Word. Reading a letter from home is never as good as sitting in the presence of our loved ones. When we cannot do that, then a letter is the best alternative. So it is with God's Word. He has spoken to us through His Word. We need to begin to listen to His voice in it.

O Thou who hast chosen to reveal Thyself to us through Thy Word, help us to study Thy Word, listening for Thy voice. Hearing Thee, help us to obey. This we pray in Jesus' name. Amen.

HIDING FROM GOD'S VOICE

And they heard the sound of the Lord God walking in the garden in the cool of the day, and the man and his wife hid themselves from the presence of the Lord God among the trees of the garden.

GENESIS 3:8

When we read the tragic story of rebellion in the Garden of Eden, most of us wind up by focusing our attention on the separation that God forced upon Adam and Eve when He thrust them forth from His presence (see Gen. 3:24). In considering this, our hearts are saddened by the barrier God placed between our ancestors and Himself.

However, if we are not careful, we shall miss a much more

important element of the story. We should never forget—although we seldom remember—that it was Adam and Eve who first separated themselves from God. In arrogant pride they had disobeyed God. But it was in abject terror that they hid from His voice as He came seeking them in the garden.

This is still the sad, tragic experience of each of us. We proudly flaunt our freedom to disobey the commands of God. Then, having done so, we are no longer able to face the judging truth of His revelation. Perhaps this is an explanation for the fact that so many of us avoid the study of God's Word.

Could it be that we are afraid of what we might find in such a study? Are we fearful of hearing God's voice of judgment upon our sins? Are we terrified by the thought that when we examine ourselves in the mirror of the Scriptures that we shall be appalled by what we see?

Some of us have become quite adept at bending the message of God so that it does not apply to us. That is one way of hiding from God's voice. But all of us regularly avoid being confronted by the demands of God by just avoiding the Bible itself.

If there is any one thing clear about the Bible, it is that it is a demanding Book. There is no way we can read God's Word without being confronted by its demands. We may choose to disobey the Bible's demands. We may also choose to ignore them. But if we have read the Bible at all, we are at least aware that God makes demands of us.

So you and I, like our primal parents, choose to avoid the demands of God by hiding from Him in the first place. And when we do not face the demands of God, we try to deceive ourselves into believing that all is well in our lives. But this is the way of death.

Unfortunately, the insidious voice of evil is always there, telling us that we can get along without God. In fact, we are told that we can be like God. This is the serpent's lie. We can never be like God on our own, even though we were made in God's image. But our sin destroys that image. It is only as God has made Himself like us, in Christ, that it is possible for His image to be restored in us.

Let us then resolve that we should no longer hide from God's demands of us. Let us search His Word, letting Him confront us, so that He can recreate us in His image through our Lord Jesus. Hiding from the voice of God is the way of darkness. Letting His voice confront us in cleansing power puts us in the light as He is in the light, and this leads us to life.

Merciful Father, give us the courage to stand in the light of Thy loving presence, that we may see both what we are and what we may become through Christ Jesus, our Lord. Amen.

HEARING THE LION'S ROAR

And he said:
"The Lord roars from Zion,
and utters his voice from Jerusalem;
the pastures of the shepherds mourn,
and the top of Carmel withers."

AMOS 1:2

"The Lion has roared;
who will not fear?
The Lord God has spoken;
who can but prophesy?"

AMOS 3:8

To the young Samuel, the voice of God came softly in the night. To the fearful Elijah, God spoke in a voice of silent quietness. But Amos marched to the beat of a different drummer. The voice of God came to him as the ear-splitting, spine-tingling roar of the lion.

What does Amos' experience have to say to us who long to hear the voice of God? Furthermore, what does his experience say to us who think that everyone should hear God speak the same way we have heard him?

The voice of God does not always come in tones of sweet

comfort. God often speaks in terms of dreadful judgment. God's message is not always one of peace and light. It may, and often does, come in terms of condemnation and punishment. Because He loves us, He speaks harshly concerning our sinful rebellion. Furthermore, because He is holy and righteous, He cannot abide unrighteousness in our lives.

Amos came to the people of Israel proclaiming God's judgment on them. But Amos' words were also aimed at condemning their complacency in the face of their sin. It was their failure to even care about their sin that was the basis of his message of judgment. It was also their insensitivity to the basic needs of those around them that aroused his great wrath.

For Amos, then, the voice of God brought neither sweetness nor light. Instead, it was something that terrified. We must never forget that there are times when the voice of God brings terror.

In addition, the voice Amos heard came in a totally different fashion from that which those around him were accustomed to. The priest of Bethel assumed that everyone must hear God in the same way that he did (see Amos 7:10-17). There was nothing in his own personal experience to explain the way Amos was acting and preaching. In consequence, Amaziah decided that Amos had not heard God's voice at all. He was wrong.

Amaziah was forced to learn the hard way that we dare not assume that our own experience with God is normative for everyone else. Not everyone in Amos' day heard God speak like a lion. The prophet Hosea heard God speak in terms of compassionate endearment. But the fact that these two men heard God speak in different tones does not invalidate either message. Rather, it points up the fact that we must be aware that God speaks in different ways to all of us. Though Hosea heard God speak in terms of tenderness while Amos heard the harsh roar of the lion, both heard the same message demanding practical righteousness from God's people. The tone was different. The message was the same. God's people must be faithful to God's purpose. It is that simple.

Help us, O Lord, to hear Thy message when it comes. Keep us from questioning the truth of a message whose tone is different from that which we have heard. Rather, help us to be obedient to Thy truth. Amen.

TRUSTING IN HIS PROMISES

God is not man, that he should lie,
or a son of man, that he should repent.
Has he said, and will he not do it?
Or has he spoken, and will he not fulfil it?
NUMBERS 23:19

Any parent learns very quickly that it is one thing to get your children to hear you and quite another to get them to obey. It should not be surprising that the same thing is true in the realm of the spiritual.

You and I may not devote our best efforts to hearing the voice of God whether it comes to us through His Word, through nature, or through His Holy Spirit. But whether or not we hear is of little consequence unless we are both willing and ready to obey His voice once we have heard it.

The problem appears to be that we do not really trust God. We are not ready to obey Him for we are not really ready to believe that the whole world is in His hands.

To the people of the Old Testament, the admonition came again and again to trust the divine voice. When God promised, it would come to pass. Their history furnished abundant evidences of this fact. Yet, in spite of this, they still found it difficult to trust Him for their future.

However, before we become too quick to criticize them for this, we need to examine our own relationship to God. We, too, have abundant testimony of the fact that God keeps His promises. His Word is both true and trustworthy. It always has been. It still is. Yet, in spite of this, we frequently face the future with grave doubts that God really will keep His Word.

This is both sad and tragic. It is sad, because it expresses a built-in attitude of doubt toward God's Word. It is tragic, because our lack of trust deprives us of many blessings and gifts that have been promised.

It would appear that we who have again and again seen how God keeps His promises should never again question God's dependability. But we do. We have not yet really learned that God's promises are trustworthy.

It is quite possible that we have become so engrossed in avoiding obeying God's commands that we have altogether missed the great and precious promises He has given us. Trust in God is the one thing the Bible demands of every person. Fortunately, it is the one thing everyone can give to God.

Trust is the doorway to a life that is more than mere existence. That trust is the key to a full, meaningful life. You and I, then, must learn to trust God's promises. Above all, it is the pathway to a relationship with God that the saints of the ages have trod. The great servants of God both within and without the Bible have trusted God's promises. If we would follow in their train, we must follow in their path of trust.

Heavenly Father, help us as obedient children to trust Thy promises given to us over the ages through the inspired recorders of Thy holy Word. Teach us to obey Thee in quiet trust as well as in active service. This we pray in the name of Jesus our Lord, who showed us by living example how to trust Thy promises. Amen.

And all Israel from Dan to Beersheba knew that Samuel was established as a prophet of the Lord. And the Lord appeared again at Shiloh, for
the Lord revealed himself to Samuel at Shiloh by the word of the Lord.
And the word of Samuel came to all Israel.

1 SAMUEL 3:20-4:1a

One of the major problems you and I have as people of God is
recognizing God's voice. Our text confronts this problem precisely.
God was speaking to Samuel. Samuel spoke to Israel. And Israel
knew that Samuel was God's spokesman.

Our difficulty is that we seem to approach the problem from
the wrong perspective. We wish to know how to determine through
whom God is speaking. The more fundamental question is: Is God
speaking to you? If you hear and share the message of God, it will
be recognized. Others will know that God is speaking through you.
But we must also recognize that though Israel knew God was
speaking through Samuel, they did not always obey. These are two
quite different matters. They always were. They still are.

We must face the situation first of all from the standpoint of
the prophet. It is our responsibility, if God speaks to us, to share
that message with His people. There is no evidence that Samuel
ever raised the question as to whether or not people would believe
that God had spoken to him. He apparently accepted his responsibility as that of sharing the truth that God had revealed to Him.
Perhaps this is a fundamental need for you and me. Rather than
questioning who else God is speaking through, perhaps we need to
be more sure that we are sharing what God speaks to us.

But this does not eliminate the other side of the issue. It
merely pushes it back one step. How do we recognize the voice of
God in the voices of His proclaimers?

Here, the answer is not so simple. For Israel, however, there
were some basic clues. Samuel's life bore witness to the truth of
his words. The person who speaks for God must be very careful
that his or her life reflects obedience to the word proclaimed. It is

easy to claim that God has spoken to you. It is quite another thing to live in such a way that people can experience God through your life.

It has been my privilege over the years to know people whose very life bore witness to the presence of God. No matter how critical the situation, when these persons came on the scene, there was a sense of both peace and serenity, as well as a sense of the very immediacy of God. It should be that way with all of us.

There is an intangible reality to the presence of God in the lives of those who hear and obey Him. It is not something that can be defined or explained. But it is no less real. The person who hears, obeys, and trusts the voice of God carries a sense of the presence of God. I recognize God's voice in their living.

Can others recognize God's voice in my life? This is no easy question. But it is one that demands an answer. God will have a difficult time being heard through your words if He cannot be seen and felt in your life.

Gracious God, we know that Thou hast spoken to us through the saints of the ages in Thy holy Word. Help us to live so that Thou might speak through us in this generation. In Jesus' name we pray. Amen.

chapter four

The Law That Demands

RELATING TO GOD

To many people in our world, religious and moral laws are considered at best to be some sort of emotional hangover from a society that has deservedly passed away. At the worst, such laws are seen as a dull denial of anything that is fun or enjoyable. Yet, such an attitude toward the ancient laws in our Bible is almost the direct opposite of that which ancient peoples had toward them. To the ancient Hebrews, there was the exuberant sound of trumpets in those laws. How are we to understand the change in attitude over the centuries? Is there a joyous ring in them or do they have no relevance in the modern world?

Consider, for example, the first of the Ten Commandments:

You shall have no other gods before me.
EXODUS 20:3

The Hebrew people had just come out of the land of Egypt, where gods were almost as numerous as people. They were about to face the various peoples of Canaan, who worshipped and served almost an equally large contingent of deities. In the midst of that ultra-religious world, they were being given what might have been considered an irreligious commandment. Simply stated, *God was the only god for them.* Instead of many gods, their loyalty and service was demanded by one God.

Now that may be interesting to a student of religion or history, but what does it really say to us? You and I do not live in a world where people serve a multiplicity of gods. In our world, the basic issue is not one God over against many gods, but one God over against none. For far too many people, the choice appears to be "none." In this kind of world, among this kind of people, does this ancient commandment have anything to say? Can we not pass it by and ignore it?

The answer is a decided "no!"

For this commandment, which demands that there should be no other gods besides "Me," clearly demands that the "Me" be served. To the ancients, this law demanded that they put away all other gods. To you and me, it just as surely demands that we must serve this God.

You and I are both expected and commanded to serve the God who acts in history to deliver His people. When we have alienated ourselves from Him through our sin and selfishness, He invades our history to seek us out and confront us. When we have chosen to ignore Him, He refuses to be ignored. When we have said our rebellious "no" to God, He has come in Christ Jesus to say "yes" to us.

We may shut Him out, but He cannot be shut up.

We may separate ourselves from Him, but we can never confine Him. Ancient men tried to confine Him to a tomb. They failed. Modern men have tried to confine Him to the ancient world. This, too, is doomed to failure.

God still comes to each of us through Christ Jesus. He comes in love and redemption, demanding that we accept Him, that we serve Him. The law demands this response from us. Love expects this response. Let us give it freely.

O Thou who didst reveal Thyself in the demanding law of ancient days, help us to respond to the same demands in this day. May we yield control of our lives to Thee in faith, serving Thee wholly. This we pray in the name of Jesus. Amen.

REJECTING THE LAW

Thus says the Lord:
"For three transgressions of Judah,
and for four, I will not revoke the punishment;
because they have rejected the law of the Lord,
and have not kept his statutes,
but their lies have led them astray,
after which their fathers walked.

AMOS 2:4

You and I can do many things with the law of God. We can reject it, ignore it, ridicule it, or obey it. God expects us to obey it. Most of us, at least those who love God, seek to do just that. Unfortunately, we frequently find ourselves too weak in the face of temptation. Then we break His law, slipping and sliding into sin.

On the other hand, there are times when we arrogantly feel that we know better than God what is best for us. It is at those times that we turn into rebels, self-confidently turning our backs on God's law. At such times, we are guilty of what Amos accused the people of doing—rejecting God's law.

To obey God's law is the way of servanthood.

To break God's law is the way of weakness.

To reject God's law is the way of rebellion.

It would appear to be the height of folly to turn our backs on God, consciously rejecting His law. So it is. Then what is it that leads us to take this pathway in life? Amos clearly placed the ultimate blame for this upon our lies, our falsehoods. In his day, he was referring to the idols of Israel. The gods the idols represented really did not exist, they just were not real. Yet the people of Israel made the foolish assumption that their idols were better than God. They were wrong. Nonetheless, it was their false, foolish trust in those idols that led them to reject the laws of God.

Although you and I do not serve the same kinds of idols those ancient peoples did, we are still led astray by our lies. The lies that cause us to reject God's law are those that spring from our own eager self-confidence. We boastfully claim that we alone are sufficient to face life. That just is not true. When crises come or when tragedy strikes, then we discover that there is something more needed within us. What we have failed to realize is that even when things are going good, when everything seems to be going our way, we still need additional strength and power. We have settled for merely living when we could have been really living. By rejecting God's law, we have not gained freedom. Rather, we have substituted something less for the best that God intends for us.

We may blithely go through life as if there were no God. But in the end, God always has the last word.

The road of rejection of the law of God is the road that always leads to alienation and isolation. Let us turn from that road and accept God's law as His good gift that leads us into real life. There is no better way. There are lots of lesser ways.

Dear God, we have discovered that Thou art our Shepherd. Help us to know that Thou hast planned the very best for us. When we have learned this, may we then accept Thy way as the good way, leading to life abundant. This we pray in the name of Him who came to save us, even while we had gone astray. Amen.

LEARNING THE LAW

I delight to do thy will, O my God;
thy law is within my heart.
PSALM 40:8

Most of us consider the heart to be the seat of the emotions. We talk of loving someone from the bottom of our hearts. To the ancient Hebrew, however, the heart was the seat of the mind, the will, and the conscience. It was with his or her heart that the Hebrew thought, and from it came the issues of life. This helps make our passage quite instructive.

The psalmist boldly stated his delight in obeying the law of God. For him, keeping God's law was no burden. Nor should it be a burden for us. Doing the good things that God expects ought to be both a joy and delight.

On the other hand, obeying the law becomes little more than a game of chance if we do not know what the law says. In order to obey the law, we must first know the law. It is there that the first step to obedience rests. Unless we know the law, we cannot keep it.

This principle is so simple that we generally forget it.

As a basis for delighting in doing God's will, the psalmist plainly claimed that God's law was in his heart. In other words, he *knew* it. He had committed it to memory. That was his secret. It should be ours.

The multiplicity of modern translations of the Bible has been both good and bad for us. It has been good, in that the words of the Scriptures have been over and over again put into the words of ordinary speech. This makes it easier to understand. But as we have been exposed to the many new translations, the variety of ways a particular verse can be (and has been) expressed makes it ever more difficult to commit that verse to memory. As soon as we get a verse memorized, we find a variation of it in some new translation. The different words may confuse us and the verse we had so carefully memorized slips from our minds.

This difficulty, however, is no excuse for our failure to commit the most meaningful parts of the Scriptures to memory. We need to settle on some translation that appears to be both true to the original and clearly expressed in modern language. And then start a program of memorization.

I had a friend who recently experienced a major heart attack. For an extended period of time he was in a coronary care unit, where he was not even allowed to hold a small Bible in his hand. During those days when he was on the margin between life and death, he both needed and wanted sustenance from the Word of God. Yet it was denied him. He sought to quote to himself the favorite passages of Scripture that had been most meaningful to him over the years. Unfortunately, he quickly ran through everything he had memorized.

If the same thing happened to you, how many verses could you recite? If we truly believe that the Bible is the revelation of God to sinful man, then it is only wise to spend some time making its message a part of our thinking. We must commit it to memory.

There is a motto in the courts of the land that ignorance of the law is no excuse. If this is true in civil matters, how much truer is it in eternal matters. God has given us His law. Let us devote ourselves to learning it. We may know God's law and not keep it. But we can never keep it if we do not know it.

O God, we know that Thou hast given life to us, and we rejoice in it. Help us to rejoice in the law Thou has given us as well. Give us both the purpose and the skill to commit Thy law to memory. Once we have learned it, help us to obey it. In Jesus' name we pray. Amen.

DELIGHTING IN THE LAW

Blessed is the man
who walks not in the counsel of the wicked,
nor stands in the way of sinners,
nor sits in the seat of scoffers;
but his delight is in the law of the Lord,
and on his law he meditates day and night.

PSALM 1:1-2

The Psalms are filled with the idea that God's law is delightful. This whole concept is quite foreign to just about every modern approach to any kind of law. Law is generally described in all sorts of ways, most of them distasteful. The very idea that law can be delightful is almost beyond our comprehension.

And yet, here it is. The bold assertion that God's law is a delight to those who serve God was the very first thought suggested by the psalmists of ancient Israel. That is at least worthy of some additional consideration.

For the psalmists, the delight of God's law at the very least rested in the fact that it protected them. The law was a fence around their life. But it was never seen as a restrictive barrier, keeping them in. Rather, God's law was usually seen as a protective barrier, keeping sin away.

Consider a man traveling alone in the wilderness. Each night, as he encamps, he builds a large fire. The light of his campfire keeps the terrors of the darkness at bay. So it is with God's law. It is the light of God's will that keeps the terrors of the unknown away from our lives.

But the law was more than this. It does more than just protect us. It also guides us. It is the light that illuminates the path of life, showing us the pitfalls to avoid, while also helping us to see the good way. It allows us to know what God expects of us. Furthermore, it also allows us to know what makes life good.

Our delight in God's law should go even beyond these things, however. God's law is a delight not merely because it protects, nor even because it guides us. His law should delight us because it strengthens us. It is the spiritual training that gives us strength for living.

The psalmist added that the godly not only delight in God's law, but that they also meditate on the law. The picture that immediately comes to my mind is an older person, going about the daily business of living. In doing so, such a person frequently mutters, seemingly talking to himself. To the psalmist, the real delight expressed here is the fact that the words that are being spoken are the words of the law.

The law of God is such a delight that it serves as a constant companion in life. This companionship shows the real joy it can bring. The Word of God, which has served as protection, guidance, and strength throughout all the days of our lives, becomes the companion to which we turn in every moment of life. That is the real delight of God's law. It has become the joy of our daily life. How wonderful!

O Thou who didst create the worlds to operate in such an orderly way that we can speak of natural law, help us to find in Thy spiritual law the same order for our own lives. Give us the wisdom to delight in Thy law, making it our companion in good times as well as in bad. May we find protection, guidance, and strength in it. This we pray in Thy holy name. Amen.

DEPENDING ON THE LAW

> A voice says, "Cry!"
> And I said, "What shall I cry?"
> All flesh is grass,
> and all its beauty is like the flower of the field.
> The grass withers, the flower fades,
> when the breath of the Lord blows upon it;
> surely the people is grass.
> The grass withers, the flower fades;
> but the word of our God will stand for ever.
> *ISAIAH 40:6-8*

You and I can surely identify with the prophet's predicament in this passage. He has sensed the divine command to proclaim a message to the world. Yet he is so disturbed by the conditions of his world and of his people that he doesn't feel that he has any real message to communicate. He has become disillusioned and cynical.

Surely we have experienced that feeling at some time or another in our lives. There come the times when we discover in ourselves and others the fact that even the very best of our accomplishments are just temporary. Furthermore, we also discover just how insecure life is. It seems as if there is nothing under the sun to which we can turn for an anchor to life.

When we have such feelings, we become most aware of the absolute need for some anchor to which we can attach our lives, lest we continue to drift or even be totally washed away by the storms of life. When we are confronted by life's complex questions, we discover that there are no certain answers within ourselves. When we are swept by life's tempests, we discover that we just do not have the inner strength to overcome them. Thus the desperate need for some kind of security confronts us. But even this itself seems to drive us even further into despair. Where are we to turn?

God had an answer for the prophet's predicament, and He has one for us. It is simply this: In the midst of life's instabilities, there is one thing that is stable—"The word of our God will stand for ever." The prophet was assured that he could build his life on the one stable thing in his experience—the Word of God. Furthermore, he could lead his people to do the same.

This assurance is also available to us. God's Word can be depended on. It can be trusted. Here is the one security to which any human life can anchor itself. It is important to note that our passage does not say that *all* of God's Word must be understood. Rather, what is required is that it be trusted.

Thus, when we are overwhelmed by life's uncertainties, we can find our certainty in God's law. He has shared something of Himself in that Word. Even when everything else in life comes loose, God's Word will stand secure. There is an anchor that we need to keep life steady, no matter what happens. This is worth shouting out to others. Our flesh may wither like the grass, but God's Word will be as fresh and beautiful tomorrow as it was yesterday. On that we can depend. That is good news. It is good news indeed.

O merciful Father, when life's experiences seem to sweep over us, overwhelming us with insecurity, and when Thou dost seem to be so far away that we cannot find Thee, help us to find both strength and security in the Word that Thou hast given us. May we learn to depend upon Thy Word, that we may find an anchor for life's storms. In Jesus' name we pray. Amen.

GOING BEYOND THE LAW

> For thou hast no delight in sacrifice;
> were I to give a burnt offering,
> thou wouldst not be pleased.
> The sacrifice acceptable to God is a broken spirit;
> a broken and contrite heart,
> O God, thou wilt not despise.
>
> *PSALM 51:16-17*

Most of us are quite familiar with the scathing attacks which both Jesus and the early Christians made upon the Pharisees. What we sometimes fail to note is that the attacks were not simply made upon the Pharisees but upon the pharisaical spirit. That pharisaic attitude becomes so involved with obedience to the letter of that law that it forgets both the intent and the spirit of the law.

Keeping the law is good. In fact, it is imperative. We are expected to obey the law, and to lead others to do the same.

However, you and I can keep the law with a bitter spirit and an unloving attitude. That is not, and never was, what God intended.

The psalmist had discovered several things about keeping the law. First, he had discovered that the law did not cover every eventuality of life. If, as we generally assume, this psalm came from David after his adultery with Bathsheba and his murder of her husband, the great king had discovered that the sacrificial law made no provision for sacrifices to cover those particular sins. The law was limited. It does not cover all life situations that might possibly arise. It does not deal with every sin or provide for every need. The law leads us to God. It does not become our god.

The psalmist had discovered that he could offer every sacrifice either suggested or commanded in the Old Testament, and his particular needs still would not be met. His only hope was to go beyond the law and throw himself on the mercy of God. The same is true for us.

We, too, discover that while the Biblical laws of life may be adequate for many needs, they are not adequate for every need. Furthermore, as we come to know the Lawgiver, we begin to apprehend the spirit of the law.

Keeping the law of God is far better than doing what is right in our own eyes. But going beyond the law to follow the Spirit of God is infinitely better than that. God's Spirit will not lead us to violate His law. Rather He leads us to discover that the life that goes far beyond the law is the life of abundance.

Keeping the law of God will lead to righteousness. But it may also lead to self-righteousness. Following God beyond His law with humility and contrition leads to a godly life. That is the kind of life God intends for us to have. Then we no longer *merely* live, we *really* live. Then we will have become not simply good, but godly.

Help us, O Lord, not only to learn to follow and to obey the demands of the law, but also to seek Thee behind, above, and beyond Thy law. May we never become mean and harsh, but may we be both eager and open to Thy will and to Thy people. May we never view Thy law as something to be attained, but as a beginning point to go beyond. This we pray in the name of Thy Son, our Lord, Jesus Christ. Amen.

---

chapter five
The Word That Illuminates

UNVEILING THE DIVINE SECRETS

> Surely the Lord God does nothing,
> without revealing his secret
> to his servants the prophets.
> The lion has roared;
> who will not fear?
> The Lord God has spoken;
> who can but prophesy?
> *AMOS 3:7-8*

I do not need to try to convince you that God speaks. You would not be reading this book if you did not believe that God speaks and that He speaks to you. You are seeking to hear God speak to you this very minute.

So we agree that God speaks and that He speaks to us. That is a good starting point.

But there is something of which both you and I need to be convinced, and that is that God does not try to keep secret from us those things that we need to know. In general, we far too frequently approach the Scriptures as if we were trying to discover some great secret God has hidden from us. In fact, the very opposite is true. We ought to be approaching the Bible as friends of God, trying to understand something He has given to us. God does not hide His message. He seeks to make it clear. Whenever we fail to comprehend God's Word, we do so because of our own ignorance or lack of understanding, not because God is keeping a secret from us.

For Amos, the message of God was like a lion's roar that reverberated through the hills into the hearts of the people. Thus, if God has so spoken and spoken so openly, it is we who have allowed the message to become confused and distorted over the years. We have allowed the barnacles, as it were, to collect on God's Word. So it is we who must seek to understand and to communicate what God has spoken.

There is a great deal written about the so-called mystery religions of the New Testament era, in which only those initiated into them knew the secrets of what their gods had said and what it meant. The God of Israel may have been a mystery, but He did not call His people to a mystery religion. Instead, He called them to hear, to heed, and to follow the open teachings concerning His will. He still does.

Of one thing Amos was absolutely sure, God might surprise His people by what He said, but He would not surprise them by doing something with no advance warning. For Amos, God's biggest surprise was that He opened up His secrets, unveiling them to His prophets, and through them to His people.

Thus God has unveiled His secrets in His Word. It is those secrets which can, will, and must illuminate our lives.

O Thou who has revealed Thyself, help us that we may seek to understand that which is open, rather than to uncover that which is hidden. Open the eyes of our minds and our hearts, that we may both hear and heed, and that we may then both share and lead in obeying Thy Word. For this we pray from the very depths of our being, in Jesus' name. Amen.

SCATTERING THE DARKNESS

And God said, "Let there be light"; and there was light. And God saw that the light was good; and God separated the light from the darkness.

GENESIS 1:3-4

In the beginning of the creation of the universe, God began with a flash of light such as the world has never seen since. Yet, in a very real sense, what God has been doing ever since that initial moment has been the same thing, creating light. He has been shining His light into our lives, scattering our darkness. And the light that He is now shining is the light of His will and purpose and the light of His love. He brings light to scatter whatever darkness envelopes us.

It is our fault if we choose to face the darkness. The light is available. It is our responsibility if we choose to dwell in the darkness, for He is the light. No darkness can extinguish light, not ever.

However, it is not only our opportunity to live in the light of God's will and love, it is also our responsibility to become light bearers, reflecting God's light into the lives of those round about us. In fact, Jesus called His disciples the light of the world. We are precisely that, not in the sense that light springs from us, but in the sense that we reflect His light. It is our task, then, to be that light, to shine His light into darkness, wherever the darkness is.

There are all kinds of darknesses that beset the human soul. There is the darkness of fear, hunger, despair, guilt, grief, and all those countless ills that the flesh is heir to. But no darkness, no matter how black it may appear, is sufficient to extinguish any glimmer of light. And the light of God does not always come in brilliant flashes. It sometimes comes with only the faint hint of a dawn to come. But that faint hint is enough. Just the smallest glimmer of light scatters the darkness.

Yet this is precisely what hope is. It is the light that keeps the darkness at bay. All the demons of the darkness, whether real or imagined, flee before the first glimmers of the light of God's love.

The terrified little boy, awakening from his nightmare, screams in the darkness from the fears that haunt his dreams. Then comes a loving parent with the light, and the terrors flee with the darkness. So it is in our spiritual pilgrimage. The terrors that haunt our darkness flee from the light that reveals God. It is God's light that keeps the darkness away.

Thus, it is up to us to live in God's light. Sometimes our darkness is no more real than the darkness that comes by keeping our eyes closed. But sometimes it is awesomely real. In either case, God offers us His light. If need be, He will help us merely open our eyes. But if necessary, He will shine His love into the very remotest corners of our fear and despair. Thus we can become people who live in the light. But we can also become light bearers and light sharers. We can scatter darkness wherever we go. Yet even then, at the very best, we only reflect the light of God. It is He who is the light.

Thou who hast both created and given light, help us to open our darkness to Thy light, that we may find joy in place of grief, hope in place of despair, and mercy in place of guilt. This we pray in the name of Him who is Thy Light to us, even Jesus our Lord. Amen.

SATISFIED WITH THE BEST

The initial verses of Genesis tell us of the mighty works of creation with which God began this universe. It is a moving and exalted piece of literature with a very profound spiritual message. There is a fascinating observation that draws the narrative to a close, but which we frequently overlook, at least in its fullest implications:

And God saw everything that he made, and behold, it was very good. And there was evening and there was morning, a sixth day.

GENESIS 1:31

We usually read that statement and rejoice in it, glad that God was pleased with what He had done. But think about it. The Bible tells us that when God completed the entire work of creation, He was satisfied. What does it take to satisfy God? He surely has the most exhaustive standards. Yet, He was pleased with the world and all that was in it.

Now that is exciting!

Yet, all too frequently, we fail to get excited about it. We read the statement, think about how wonderful it is, and then quickly forget all about it. It is almost as if we were yawning at this great truth.

Later on, as we proceed about the business of living, we foul up somewhere, making a wrong choice, doing an evil deed, hurting someone who loves us, and then we seek to excuse ourselves by shrugging our shoulders, and saying, "But I'm only human."

So what?

I need to remind myself that when God made me "only human," He was satisfied. You must remind yourself that when God made you "only human," He was pleased. "Only human" is precisely what God intended us to be and is precisely what pleased Him. Therefore, being "only human" is no excuse for not being what God intends us to be.

We frequently look at ourselves and think what a sad job of creating God did. Now we do not usually put it quite that boldly. But we do think that if we had been in charge of creation, we could have made us a bit better than we are.

Somewhere along the way, we need to rescue an expression from the garbage heap of language. We need to transform the idea that being "only human" is an excuse for failure. Rather, we must recognize it as a *reason* for achievement, for success, for obedience, for pleasing God, and for helping others. We *are* human. But that is precisely what God made us to be. We are not and were not intended to be angels. And when God saw our humanity, He was pleased. That was very good.

When we look into our mirrors, we need to say, "Hey, God is pleased with me. He liked the way He made me." Maybe therefore I ought to be pleased with myself as He made me. This does not mean that I should be pleased with my sins, for this is what I have done for myself. But I should be pleased with the way God made me. This is something to be happy about. I am the "me" God made. And that was very good.

Merciful Father, help us to be satisfied with what Thou hast made us. Forgive us when we have failed in developing ourselves, but help us become what Thou hast made us to be. Help us to find acceptance with Thee and to accept ourselves, through Jesus Christ our Lord we pray. Amen.

DISCOVERING OTHER COMPANIONS

Yet I will leave seven thousand in Israel,
all the knees that have not bowed to Ba'al,
and every mouth that has not kissed him.

1 KINGS 19:18

Immediately preceding our text, Elijah had won his great victory over the prophets of Baal on top of Mount Carmel. While still savoring his victory, Elijah received Jezebel's threat that she was going to kill him. Terrified, the prophet turned and ran all the way to Mount Sinai. There he was confronted by God's still, small voice, which spoke the words in our text.

The message here, of course, is rather obvious. Elijah was feeling completely alone. He felt that he was the only one around who was committed to doing God's will. God responded to Elijah that he was not alone. God had lots of other servants out there.

Sometimes, being a Christian becomes a frightening experience. Then we often begin to feel that we, too, are all alone. In a large Christian assembly recently, an elderly woman walked into the auditorium, looked at the throngs of people, and burst out crying. Through her tears, she said to the bystanders, "I never knew that there were that many others!" She had come from a very small church and had just never dreamed that there could be that many Christians in one place. She was overflowing with tears of joy.

There are many times when we just need to back off and remember that we are not alone. Now, we all know that God is with us. That is not what I mean. I am speaking of being alone from a human standpoint. There are others out there. The fellowship of Christians is one of the sweetest things we can enjoy on this earth. The early Christians caught the attention of the world by their shared love. So should we.

When you feel utterly alone, turn to your fellow Christians. The fellowship of others can be found in a church. They may differ from you theologically, but they will reach out to you in love.

We must never forget that we are part of a fellowship. But this idea cuts two ways. Not only must we seek for fellowship from those who love God, we must offer fellowship to them as well. St. Peter's Basilica in Rome is designed with two massive colonnades, which reach out in partial semicircles from the main building. They symbolically depict the open arms reaching out to all humanity. Thus, we must also be aware of the need to reach out, to welcome the stranger who is within our gates.

We are not alone. We must not stay alone.

There are others who are walking the path of life with us, seeking to be both faithful and loyal to Christ. We must walk together. In the beginning, God saw that it was not good for man to be alone, so God has placed us in a new relationship of love, the Church. Let us find our comfort and strength therein.

Gracious God, may we find our strength both from Thee and from those around us who call Thee Lord. May we truly experience the love that shows us we are not alone. In that love, may we know the joy of being fellow servants, fellow disciples, and fellow pilgrims. This we pray in the name of Him who came to show us that we are not alone, even Jesus our Lord. Amen.

BASKING IN GOD'S WORD

The secret things belong to the Lord our God;
but the things that are revealed belong to us
and to our children for ever,
that we may do all the words of this law.
DEUTERONOMY 29:29

Far more often than should be, I get the impression that many of us are trying to discover the secrets of God, those things that He has reserved to Himself. The sad truth is that there is every indication that when we do this sort of thing, we actually fail to do those things that He has already revealed to us. Could it be that we are seeking to penetrate God's future in order to avoid obeying Him in the present? I do not know. But I do know that we are being told here that it is our privilege to bask in the revealed Word of God.

Have you ever had the experience of coming home tired, dirty, and perhaps cold, and just taking the time and opportunity of leaning back and relaxing in a tub of hot water? At such a time, you just soak as long as you can, rejoicing in the warm, cleansing, relaxing water. Somehow, I get that image here of God's people leaning back and basking in His revelation. They appear to be immersing themselves in His Word.

Now that is a joy of which we do not take advantage very often. It is a wonderful thing just to sit back and relax, listening to God speak to us. It is a shame that we let our lives get so cluttered with demands on our time and energies that even when we turn to God's Word, we are still under pressure. Church workers are under the pressure of preparing another sermon or another Bible study lesson. We may simply be under the pressure of just getting our daily devotions done, so that we can get on with the business of living.

We sometimes allow the pressures of serving God to force us into the neglect of a simple enjoyment of God through His revelation, a treasure that has been entrusted to us. Unfortunately, the treasure of God's Word has become so commonplace that we may be taking it for granted. Even the multiplicity of translations may have become a handicap. We have so many Bibles around that we have lost the excitement of possessing the very revelation of God Himself. Here is a message from the One who created this universe, a Word from the One who has both created and redeemed you, and who has loved you from the very depths of His being. With such a Word, we still just go flippantly through it. How tragic!

Our clocks tell us that it is time for our daily devotions, so we reach for the Bible and let it fall open and begin to read. Or even when we have some system, we just read a few verses, pray, and go on about our business, never pausing to ponder what we have read. How ridiculous!

When I receive a letter from a friend, I immediately read every word. I do not just read a sentence or two and lay it aside, planning on reading two more lines tomorrow. When I get the letter, I read it from beginning to end. Should I not do the same with God's Word? Here I have a letter penned by the hand of Paul, or a sermon preached by the mouth of Isaiah, and yet I seldom read more than a paragraph at a time. You and I need to recapture the joy of reading God's Word. It is His message to us. Let us hear it.

Help us, O Lord, not merely to hear Thy Word, but to rejoice in hearing it. Help us to learn to apply Thy Word to our lives, not merely searching the Scriptures, but being searched by them, in Jesus' name we pray. Amen.

SHINING IN MERCY

The Lord is my light and my salvation;
whom shall I fear?
The Lord is the stronghold of my life;
of whom shall I be afraid?

PSALM 27:1

There are a lot of theological, "church" terms we Christians use that really do not communicate anything to the contemporary world. This is tragic since the Bible was originally written in the language of the ordinary people. The fact that our religious language does not communicate is not the fault of the Bible but of the words that we choose to describe its teachings.

Let us consider, for example, the term *salvation* in our passage. To the ancient Hebrew, this term referred to deliverance from anything that oppressed. It was used to describe deliverance from one's enemies, from suffering, or from the evils of life. The point is, when the Old Testament Hebrews spoke of salvation, they were not thinking of some otherworldly experience, but one that was intensely of *this* world. God was the One who delivered them from whatever troubled them.

That was an amazing statement of confidence.

It still is today.

Ultimately, the confidence of the psalmist rested in the fact that God illuminated the dark night of despair in life. He could— and would—deliver from any trouble. Now this was a light for life. It illuminated his pathway as it illuminates ours. We can have confidence in God.

But this statement of faith drives us to another question. If we can have confidence in God, and we can, how can such confidence be possible? This certainly demands an answer. It also deserves one.

The answer is profound in its simplicity. You and I can have confidence in God because of His mercy. We have nothing to fear because God loves us, forgives us, and restores us. The ultimate enemy from which we are delivered is our own sin and guilt. God delivers us from evil through His free pardon. We neither deserve His pardon nor can we earn it. Yet He delivers us anyway. It is this that gives us genuine confidence.

Now that is real light. When I am ensnared by my own sin and guilt, God's mercy shines into my life. This is the ultimate light of God, which shines into every dark part of my life.

When you and I look at God, we see the light of His mercy

shining from His face. It truly illuminates the darknesses that have surrounded us. For the psalmist, this was the basis of his confidence. It was enough for him. It should be enough for us.

The world may not understand our use of the term *salvation*. But it will surely understand God's merciful deliverance. He loves us. That is understandable. It is a message that needs to be shared. It is a message that we can share. And it is a message that gives us confidence in life. God will deliver His people from their oppressors.

Merciful Father, teach us so much of Thy love that we do not fear Thee, so much of Thy mercy that we do not hide from Thee, and so much of Thy power that we do not despise our weakness. This we pray through Jesus Christ, who came to bring Thy mercy to us. Amen.

---

chapter six

The Servant Who Obeys

INVITED TO OBEY

Thus says the Lord:
"Stand by the roads, and look,
and ask for the ancient paths,
where the good way is; and walk in it,
and find rest for your souls."

JEREMIAH 6:16

Every generation seems to think that it is at a major crossroads of history. Politicians, educators, and preachers all appear to consider that the present moment (whatever it may be) is the supreme moment of decision, a crossroads that will affect history forever afterward. Before we poke too much fun at such attitudes, let us remember that this is, in a real sense, very true. Life is always at a crossroads. The decision and the actions of this present moment do shape our future. This is inescapable. Yesterday affected today, and today affects tomorrow.

In facing this fact, God offers us some guidance in making the decisions and performing the actions that shape our future. We dare not ignore this.

The first step in making today's decisions is to examine the alternatives. No decision should ever be made without considering the options open to us. Sadly, many decisions are so made. For a person wandering in a strange land, the various forks that a road takes may offer some guidance by a simple examination. Which road has the deepest ruts, which is the most heavily traveled? Which is wider, less rugged, more easily followed? These are the kinds of things that can be seen by examination. But how about the pathways of life? Can we find some of the same things by examination? Well, we can at least learn from the obvious experiences of others who have faced similar choices and made similar decisions. We must seek others' advice.

But, we must also go beyond simply examining the options. The second step toward becoming an obedient servant is to ask for the "ancient paths." Our generation is enamored with the new. We have assumed that just because something is new and modern it is better. That is just not necessarily so. Perhaps the experience of the years can serve as a guide to us. We must at least give consideration to it. The faith of our fathers has stood the test of time. What is the testimony of those who have gone before?

However, old is not necessarily better, either. So our third step in this process is to determine what the "good way" is. Here, God's Word can serve as a guide. Also, the testimony and the witness of God's saints offer aid. Yet even this is not sufficient. All of this investigating and questioning lead nowhere if we do not take the final step.

The fourth step is simply to "walk in it." We must obey God's will once we have discovered it. Finding the best way accomplishes nothing if we do not go that way. God calls us to the best way, so that we may live a life of obedient service. The end result of that life is absolute refreshment. That is what God intends for us. We can find nothing better. We should settle for no less.

O Thou who didst lead Israel through the wilderness into the land of promise, lead us through the wilderness of our lives into that rich, full existence Thou hast planned for us. Help us to follow Thee wherever Thou dost lead. This we pray in Jesus' holy name, Amen.

REQUIRING OBEDIENCE

"With what shall I come before the Lord,
and bow myself before God on high?
Shall I come before him with burnt offerings,
with calves a year old?"
He has showed you, O man, what is good;
and what does the Lord require of you
but to do justice, and to love kindness,
and to walk humbly with your God?

MICAH 6:6,8

There is a spiritual nature inherent in our hearts that makes us want to worship and serve God. Yet, the problem that has beset us from the earliest dawn of time down to the present is "How can we come into the presence of God?" It is a question that needs an answer. It is a question that also deserves an answer.

From mankind's earliest days on earth, there has been the sense in our hearts that some sort of sacrifice must please God. Therefore, the costlier and better the sacrifice, the more it must please Him, or so we have thought. But experience has shown that, although this might at times make us feel better, it does not always work.

So people decided that it was not merely the quality of the sacrifice that was important, but the manner in which it was offered. If we brought our gifts to God with more honor, being more precise in the ritual of how we made the offering, surely this would accomplish our purposes. Then at last we would be able to enter into His presence. But the passing years have shown the inadequacy of this idea also. The difficulty of finding God was made no less difficult by the highly developed rituals of sacrifice.

It is precisely at this point that the prophet Micah stepped in with his words of guidance. He made four simple statements. They are as true today as they were when he spoke them. Given the frustrations of trying to enter into the presence of God, Micah presented his program of spiritual growth and enlightenment.

First, God has not left us without guidance. He has revealed His will to us. It is as we study and consider His will and purposes that we find the way into His presence.

Second, God demands that those who would find Him must first be just in their dealings with others. We cannot hope to find acceptance with God when we have mistreated those whom God loves. It is that simple.

Third, we are to "love kindness." This is a very difficult expression to translate simply. It literally means to enjoy the doing of the acts of loyalty and merciful kindness to others that God enjoys doing for us. We cannot expect to come into His presence when do not enjoy what He does.

Fourth, the last step in entering into God's presence is to pattern our lives after Him in meekness. We dare not approach God with pride or arrogance. Rather, we must come into His presence filled with awe and wonder that He has allowed us to live with Him. He has become our Companion for life. We discover God as we deal with others in the same manner He deals with us.

This is God's requirement of us.

O Thou who hast come to us in Thy love and law, help us to live in Thy presence through serving others as Thou hast served them. May we truly walk in Thy way, showing others by the deeds of our lives that we belong to Thee. This we pray through Him who most completely fulfilled this demand, Jesus Christ our Lord. Amen.

FOLLOWING THE GOOD WAY

It is easy to try to overcomplicate the way we serve God. Whether we develop an elaborate ritual of sacrifice or create a long list of things we should or should not do, not one of these man-made approaches really brings us to God. The good way seems to be as illusive as ever. Our problem is usually the simple fact that we still seek to come to God in *our* terms, rather than on *His*. God spoke through Hosea to tell of His way. This is the good way to the good life.

> For I desire steadfast love and not sacrifice,
> the knowledge of God, rather than burnt offerings.
>
> *HOSEA 6:6*

"Steadfast love" is a term that carries a very rich meaning in the Hebrew Old Testament. It includes loyalty, commitment, mercy, kindness, and love. All these things collectively and each of these things individually describe what God wants from us. He has loved us and given Himself for us. In return, He expects this kind of response.

But do we give it, really? Are we really loyal to God? Do we offer Him a love that is anything more than a superficial emotional response?

It is the loyalty of our own committed life that God expects, rather than the offering of any or all possessions. This in no way implies that He despises our offerings, but that they must come from a dedicated life.

Far too frequently we have offered God nothing but a warmed-over emotional response to some kind of deep inner longing within us. Instead, we should give Him our dedicated devotion because of what and who He is. Stedfast love is the love that endures no matter what. It is the love that serves regardless of the difficulties. It is the love that is loyal when everyone else in the world seems to be unfaithful. But this is not all that God expects from us. There is more.

God also expects "the knowledge of God" from His people. This is the translation of a Hebrew idiom that can easily be misunderstood if we are not careful. In the Old Testament, the word translated "knowledge" does not mean a mere collection of facts that we have learned. Rather, it means that which we have learned through the most intimate experience. Thus, "the knowledge of

God" is what we know about God through a personal relationship with Him.

A personal, experiential relationship with God is more important than all the rituals we have performed. It is more important than all the creeds we have learned or signed. God expects us to live our lives in a personal relationship with Him.

The terms by which His relationship with us is described in the Bible all express an intimate personal relationship. Consider these for a moment. He is Father; we are His children. He is husband; we are His betrothed. He is Shepherd; we are His sheep. The list could be enlarged. But it clearly points up the fact that God is most fully known through our relationship with Him. Let us then live in that relationship, enjoying the loving fellowship of God Himself, serving Him through devoted, loyal love.

Thou hast called us unto Thyself, O Lord, and we would live in that fellowship, basking in the warmth of Thy love, becoming what Thou wouldst have us to be. May we live in relationship with Thee, as Thine own Son did while on earth. This we pray in His name. Amen.

THE WISDOM OF OBEYING

Whoever is wise, let him understand these things;
whoever is discerning, let him know them;
for the ways of the Lord are right,
and the upright walk in them,
but transgressors stumble in them.
HOSEA 14:9

Nobody wants to be called a fool. Even more to the point, no one wants to act like or to be a fool. Yet, our folly is that we do not behave as if we were wise, at least as we consider matters of the spirit.

The person who is wise must understand that a good person is (and must be) a godly person. In our contemporary society, a great deal is based on the profit motive. Before making the effort to do what is right, most people want to know, "What's in it for me?" That is a tragic development of life. The way of wisdom is goodness for goodness' sake.

You and I should be good just because it is the thing to do. It is the wise way. It is the way of God.

Furthermore, the way of wisdom recognizes that God is good. His acts are good and His ways are good. Far too frequently, modern people want to sit in judgment of God. There is nothing more foreign to the Biblical way of thinking. We cannot sit in judgment of God. He sits in judgment of us. Only God is good.

But even more to the point, whatever God does is good. It is at this point that many stumble. Faith falters at the so-called problem of God's goodness. But the problem is not one of God's goodness but of our own lack of understanding.

Our knowledge is limited. We do not like to admit that, but it is true. Furthermore, our understanding and reasoning abilities are limited. We do not like to admit this either, but it is also true.

What we do need to face and to admit is that God's ways are good. His ways are beyond our comprehension. Yet, we are expected to follow Him, walking in fellowship with Him. That is the essence of faith. Even when I do not understand either God or His ways, I am still called to trust Him. I am also called upon to live by faithfulness as well as by faith. I must trust, but the trust is expected to result in a concrete demonstration of my faith. There is no lesser way.

God calls upon us to obey Him, in order to show our trust. "But," you might say, "doesn't God know that I trust Him?" Of course He does. The call to a faithful life is for our benefit as well as for others. It is for others that they may see the visible results of our trust. It is for us, that we may give concrete action to the words we profess.

So, for the Biblical faith, the way of wisdom is the way of obedience. And that obedience is based on our trust that God is good. That visible faithfulness gives light to our world, illuminating the lives of others. That is our calling.

Gracious God, we know that Thou hast called us to faith, and we have offered that faith to Thee. Give us the strength to demonstrate our faith by the way we live, walking in the way that Thou hast commanded. This we pray in the name of Jesus Christ. Amen.

OBEYING FOR OTHERS' GOOD

Now the Lord said to Abram, "Go from your country and your kindred and your father's house to the land that I will show you. And I will make of you a great nation, and I will bless you, and make your name great, so that you will be a blessing. I will bless those who bless you, and him who curses you I will curse; and by you all the families of the earth shall bless themselves.

GENESIS 12:1-3

Not many of us have the opportunity of performing an act that will really change the course of history. Just suppose for a moment you were given a chance to do something that could forever afterward be called a great watershed of human history.

Would you do it?

Your first thought might be of the fame and prestige that would come your way by performing such an act. Then, just consider the rewards of doing such an act. There would certainly be all sorts of ways to turn your fame into financial reward.

But, as you think of all this, remember that the opportunity also involves risk and danger. There is a very real chance that you might be killed. You must carefully weigh both the risks and dangers. Now, what about it? Would you still do it?

The decision obviously becomes much harder now. It is not as easy to be a volunteer when you carefully consider all the risks involved. By and large, most of us are not really very brave when it comes to facing real dangers.

Now, against that background, consider the call of Abraham (or Abram, as he was first known). What was it that led him to obey God's call to leave everything behind? Obviously, we do not really know. It may have been simply a desire to obey God. It may have been the desire for all the blessings that God promised. But it may have been the desire to help others; for Abraham was promised that, if he obeyed God, others would benefit.

Think about that for a moment. Would you have faced all the risks, braved all the dangers, merely for the purpose of helping unknown people in an unknown land. For most of us, this is highly unlikely. For most of us, it is hard enough to face real danger when our motive is the goal of simply helping others.

Now, think again. Abraham's response is precisely the response made by any missionary who goes out from his or her home in response to God's call. This is the response made by all people who set forth to serve God wherever He calls them. To the world, it is both strange and inconceivable that anyone should be willing to go to the ends of the earth for God, that others might come to know Him. But that is precisely the task to which God calls us. Amazingly, that is precisely why we go.

Great God of all peoples, send us to those who have not heard of Thy love or come to experience Thy mercy. We offer ourselves to Thee as servants, willing to go to the ends of the earth for the benefit of those who have never known Thee. This we pray through Jesus, Thy Son, our Lord, who came to show us Thy love. Amen.

DELIGHTING IN OBEDIENCE

And Samuel said,
"Has the Lord as great a delight in burnt offerings
and sacrifices, as in obeying the voice of the Lord?
Behold, to obey is better than sacrifice,
and to hearken than the fat of rams."

1 SAMUEL 15:22

It is a strange, but perhaps not unexpected, fact that most of us approach God as we might deal with some very important person. Our concern is generally how to please or satisfy Him. Yet, at the same time, we are always seemingly involved in trying to impress Him.

We act as if God might be impressed with our gifts, or by our loyalty, or by our regular attendance at worship. We are trying to impress God with our "busyness" and our importance; and how flattered He should be by the things we might do that are "showy."

How sad.

Such an attitude clearly demonstrates that we have misunderstood His concerns. In fact, it shows that we have really misunderstood His very nature. God is not impressed with us. He *knows* us. He made us what we are and has seen what we have become.

It is far more important for us to ask, "What is it that pleases God?" than to ask, "What is it that impresses God?" You and I need to give our time and attention to doing that which gives Him pleasure and delight.

That is quite simple.

God expects us to obey Him. A loving parent is most pleased by an obedient son or daughter. God, our spiritual Father, is delighted by our obedience. It is this that shows both our desire to please Him and our desire to serve Him.

The fact is, God's commands are designed to help us find a life of quality. It is His expectations that help us to become the very best person we can be. God is pleased most when we reach our highest fulfillment. Our attempts to impress God are designed to make Him think we are something which we are not. Our attempts to obey God show what we really are and are becoming.

God, our loving Father, desires nothing but the very best for us. His purposes help us to attain that "very best." It is as we obey Him—and only as we obey Him—that we begin to fulfill His plans for our lives.

Therefore, if we as God's children really desire to please Him, we can do it by obeying Him. God loves you and me. He is most delighted when we become wholly what we can be. God desires me to be the very best "me" that is possible. This is attained through obedience to His will. Then He rejoices with me at what I have become.

That is God's delight. It should be yours and mine as well.

Merciful Father, we thank Thee that Thou dost desire the very best for us and hast planned that in Thine holy will. We beseech Thee that Thou wouldst help us not to seek to impress Thee, so much as to delight Thee through our obedience. Help us to be faithful children, through Jesus our Lord, in whose name we pray. Amen.

chapter seven

The Faith That Shows

LIVING YOUR FAITH

The word of the Lord came to me: "You shall not take a wife, nor shall you have sons or daughters in his place. . . . Do not enter the house of mourning, or go to lament or bemoan them; . . . You shall not go into the house of feasting to sit with them, to eat and drink."

JEREMIAH 16:1-2, 5, 8

How does the world know that you have been with God?

That is an honest question and it deserves an honest answer. It is easy to proclaim to the world that you are a Christian. It is easy to insist that anyone can know that you are a Christian because you have your name on the roll of a particular church or because you regularly attend that church. But is that really enough?

The answer, obviously, is: "No, that is not enough."

Then, what *is* enough? Can we arrive at a better answer?

Jeremiah was given a better answer. The details of the answer are not as important as the nature of the answer. Jeremiah was a prophet in the last, dark days of the Kingdom of Judah. He had been proclaiming a coming judgment that was going to fall upon the guilty nation of Judah. In the midst of that proclamation, God announced to him that his life had better be consistent with his preaching.

Jeremiah had been declaring that the coming judgment was

going to be so bad that there would no longer be anything worth celebrating in the national life. If he really believed that, then he had better not allow himself to go to any parties. God expected his life to give evidence that he believed what he had proclaimed.

Furthermore, Jeremiah had also announced that the coming judgment was going to be so horrible, that it would be better to be dead than to have to face it. God warned that if he really believed that, then there was no sense mourning for the dead. If Jeremiah's message were true, then the dead were better off than the living. Also, if Jeremiah really believed his own message, then he should not bring children into the world to face the horrors he had envisaged. And the responsibilities of having a wife would distract him from the centrality of his task, if he really believed that his message was Judah's last hope.

In simple terms, Jeremiah was being told that it was imperative that his life demonstrate that he really believed his message. The same is true of us. The only way the world really knows what we believe is by our living demonstrations. We are called upon to let our faith show through our actions. The real test of faith, then, is not words, but deeds. Faith shows in the way we drive, the way we treat our fellow laborers, the way we serve our communities, the manner in which we act at recreational events, the kinds of things we do for our own relaxation, as well as every other aspect of our lives. It matters little what words we use to describe our faith. What is important is how it affects our lives. The faith that shows is the faith that we really hold. There is no other.

Almighty God, help us to be able to show by our lives that we have devoted ourselves to Thy service. May we give a living demonstration of our love for Thee and for Thy people. Help us to be doers of Thy Word. This we pray in Jesus' name. Amen.

FINDING GOD IN GOOD

Seek the Lord and live, lest he break out like fire
in the house of Joseph, and it devour,
with none to quench it for Bethel, ...
See good, and not evil, that you may live;
and so the Lord, the God of hosts,
will be with you, as you have said.
Hate evil, and love good,
and establish justice in the gate; ...

AMOS 5:6, 14-15

Sometimes those of us who are in vocational ministry in a local church become very pious about people's need to seek God. We can (and do) speak about this in tones that are so pious that our voices seem to drip with honey from the altar of God. Unfortunately, our very piousness may turn people away from the God we preach.

The prophet Amos was much more practical than this. He, too, urged his people to seek God. But he spelled it out for them in quite practical terms. The prophet from Tekoa bluntly announced that seeking God is begun by seeking good. Now those of us living on this side of the Cross might misunderstand the prophet's emphasis. He was not speaking of seeking God for salvation by doing good, as we might. He is speaking of seeking God insofar as the doing of God's will. For him, the way to life was the way of obedience. Furthermore, the way of obedience was the way of doing good.

It really became quite simple to Amos. Hate evil. Love good. However, lest anyone fail to grasp his meaning, he went even further. You and I can show that we hate evil and love good by establishing justice in our communities. It was not enough for him that people should simply be just. They must lead their communities to be just. No community, state, or nation can endure that does not deal fairly with everybody. Both the lower and upper social levels must experience the same justice in our communities.

Amos' proclamation was rooted and grounded in the basic practicalities of daily life. He left the theoretical or theological concerns to others. His concern was that our theology must show in our social ethics. If it did not, it was bad theology. This is still true.

Isn't it strange that we still have so much trouble with this? Yet how often, when we become concerned about social matters, we are told that we are meddling, having abandoned the Gospel. For Amos, whatever good news there was in his proclamation, it was that God's people were to be those who sought for good in personal, daily relationships. They also sought to make their community into a just and fair society. It was that practical for him. It should also be for us.

Help us, O Lord, that we may learn to practice your will by dealing righteously with everyone around us. May we never be content to separate life into secular and sacred areas, but may we live it wholly under Thy direction, seeking Thee in what is good, and finding Thee through obedience. This we pray in the name of Jesus Christ, our Lord. Amen.

PUTTING YOUR MONEY
WHERE YOUR MOUTH IS

Jeremiah said, "The word of the Lord came to me: Behold, Hanamel the son of Shallum your uncle will come to you and say, 'But my field which is at Anathoth, for the right of redemption by purchase is yours.' . . .

"And I bought the field at Anathoth from Hanamel my cousin, and weighed out the money to him, seventeen shekels of silver."

JEREMIAH 32:6-7, 9

Many people find great difficulty in seeing anything spiritual in money or its use. This concept is quite foreign to the Bible. Money was a very real part of life. As such, it was the concern of all those who sought to relate their whole life to God.

In the historical period just prior to our passage, Jeremiah had suddenly been given a new message to preach. Now he was able to offer hope to Judah's people instead of the doom that he had been announcing for so long. His new theme was not that they would escape judgment, but that they would eventually come back from the exile they were about to enter.

However, few people were really able to believe his message of hope, for the armies of Babylon actually had the city of Jerusalem under siege. Every direction the people of Jerusalem looked from the walls of the city, all they could see were the armies of Babylon. The doom was now so certain that they were not able to see any hope beyond.

At that point, Jeremiah's cousin Hanamel bluntly asked the prophet to buy his farm at Anathoth. The reason behind the request is quite easy to identify. Anathoth was already under the control of the armies of Nebuchadnezzar. Thus, as far as Hanamel was concerned, his farm at Anathoth was worthless. He also believed that he was about to be carried off into captivity. Since Jeremiah was saying there was hope beyond the captivity, Hanamel was offering his field to Jeremiah. The young man decided that he had rather have the money and let Jeremiah have the land, since the prophet claimed to believe that the land would have value again. Basically, what he was saying to Jeremiah was, "Put your money where your mouth is."

This was a clear call to Jeremiah once again to demonstrate his faith. If he believed that Israel was going to come back to the land, then he ought to be willing to invest his own funds in the land.

You and I, as servants of the Lord Jesus, need to learn something at this point. The world waits to see if we are willing to put our money where our mouths are. It is easy to profess a belief in world missions. The question is, how much do we give to missions?

It is easy to decry the problems of world hunger. But the real issue is, what are we investing in feeding the hungry, or even in helping them to feed themselves?

Talk is always cheap. But the world waits to see if we are willing to invest our money in carrying out those tasks and in meeting those needs that we claim to be of utmost importance. The real question about my use of financial resources is simply this: Am I willing to put my money where my mouth is?

Dear God, help us to be just as eager to use our money for the needs of the world as we are to talk about those needs. Grant to us the faith and commitment that we may truly give to meet the needs of the world. Keep us from being possessed by our possessions. This is our prayer through Thy Son, Jesus Christ, our Lord. Amen.

DEMONSTRATING LIFE'S CHOICES

See, I have set before you this day life and good, death and evil. If you obey the commandments of the Lord your God which I command you this day, by loving the Lord your God, by walking in his ways, and by keeping his commandments and his statutes and his ordinances, then you shall live and multiply, and the Lord your God will bless you in the land which you are entering to take possession of it.

DEUTERONOMY 30:15-16

It is quite easy to play a game that most of us play when we come to a passage like this. Usually we say, "Oh, that's in the Old Testament, and since we no longer live under the law, we can ignore this."

Granted, New Testament Christians no longer live under the

law in the sense that obedience to the law is the one and only way to salvation, to a right relationship with God. But at the same time, there is a message here that cannot be dismissed so glibly, a message we need to hear.

Life is always filled with choices. Decisions are the stuff out of which life's patterns are set and by which its limits are drawn. Good and evil, life and death, this or that, here or there—these are all decisions that must be made. Where are you going to go? What are you going to do? What are you going to be? Whom are you going to serve? Choices, choices, choices; these are unavoidable choices. They cannot be escaped. This is the lesson confronting us in this passage.

Some choices are easy and not so important. Others are more difficult and much more significant. Life's ultimate choices are the most difficult of all and carry the most serious consequences. It may not be easy to decide between a hot fudge sundae and a strawberry soda, but with many things, you can change your mind the next time. It is not at all easy to decide on your life's vocation or the person whom you are going to marry. These are destiny-shaping decisions, and they are never easily changed. Once made, your life will never be the same again.

Making such choices is not easy. We make our choices by a variety of means, going all the way from flipping a coin, to asking others for advice, to analyzing the options and making the decision, to agonizing for days in prayer. Usually, how we make the choice depends on what is in the balance.

At the same time, we must face the fact that frequently it is all those little, seemingly unimportant choices about which we seldom think and even more seldom pray that ultimately determine what we become. How often people say, "I never intended my life to end up like this." They may not have, but their choices for years have been pointing in that direction.

It is quite important, then, to determine early in life the goal toward which you wish to direct your life. Then, when little choices come, you won't have to stop and think, "Is this good or bad?" "Is it important or unimportant?" The only question that will need to be answered is, "Does it help me reach my ultimate goal in life?" If it doesn't, then you can simply pass it by with no other thought and no regret. When we live life this way, then the pathway has already been set, the way has already been determined. Then I can look at the path of my life and see where it has been leading. What I did yesterday and the day before have clearly demonstrated the path I am following today. Thus my end will be no surprise.

Help us, O Lord, that we may face life's choices, having made the ultimate decision about the path of our lives. Keep us from being turned aside by lesser things. In Jesus' name we pray. Amen.

TRUSTING IN THE FACE OF DOUBT

When Abraham was commanded to sacrifice Isaac, his only son, he set forth with his son and some of his servants. Upon their arrival at Mount Moriah, Abraham and Isaac left the servants behind and began their ascent of the mountain.

> And Isaac said to his father Abraham, "My father!" And he said, "Here am I, my son." He said, "Behold, the fire and the wood; but where is the lamb for a burnt offering?" Abraham said, "God will provide himself the lamb for a burnt offering, my son." So they went both of them together.
>
> GENESIS 22:7-8

Christians speak a great deal about faith. We also talk a great deal about the "assurance of our faith." It seems to me, though, that the biggest test of faith comes in the time of doubt, not of assurance. If I am assured of something, it requires very little faith to believe in it. When I doubt something, but trust it anyway, that is real faith.

Consider Isaac for a moment. He was not naive. He had been

around long enough to know about child sacrifice as it was practiced in his day. And he knew that he was the oldest son of Abraham and Sarah, the one who belonged supremely to God, according to ancient Near Eastern thought. From this background he saw the wood and fire and questioned where the lamb was. Deep in his own being, he knew where the lamb was. *He* was the lamb!

But then, his father, whom he both loved and trusted, said that God would provide a lamb for the sacrifice. Now what?

I wonder just what Isaac was thinking as he and his father climbed that mountain. There must have been a hope that his father knew what he was talking about, that God did have another victim available. Yet none was visible. He had to be beset by doubt. In spite of this, he walked on, obediently accompanying his father. He could have run away. There was no way in which old Abraham could have caught young Isaac. But he did not run. He followed on, in trusting obedience.

Of course, when they reached the top of the hill, Abraham bound Isaac. Can you imagine trying to tie up a youth when he did not want to be tied up? Here again is evidence of Isaac's obedience.

But, there is also Abraham in this story. He knew that he was to sacrifice Isaac. At the same time, he also knew that God had promised to him a multitude of descendants *through Isaac.* Now, how could Abraham do the one and believe the other? Faith demanded that he trust God. Harsh reality pointed out the utter folly of that. What was going on in Abraham's mind? Whatever else was going on, there is one thing they both had in common—and that is faith! Isaac was trusting his father. Yet he knew in his heart that there was something rotten with the whole story. Abraham was trusting God. Yet somehow it all did not fit together. They both knew that something just didn't make sense.

This was the real test of faith. It is immaterial that we know the end of the story. The point is that they didn't. What do you do when it appears that what is happening is contradictory to what God has promised? With Abraham and Isaac, the answer was simply, "Hang in there." "Hold on to your faith." The real test of faith is what we do at such a time. Can we hang in there? We must, for there is no other way.

Help us, O Lord, to trust Thee when life makes no sense. Give us the grace to believe you fully. In Jesus' name we pray. Amen.

MAKING FAITH VISIBLE

> He who withholds kindness from a friend
> forsakes the fear of the Almighty.
>
> JOB 6:14

What is a saint? There are many definitions given, which vary all the way from the official definitions of the Roman Catholic Church to the technical definition of an unabridged dictionary. Perhaps one of the better explanations is that given by the little child who had viewed the saints portrayed in the stained-glass windows of her church. She said simply, "A saint is someone who lets the light shine through."

What a profound truth is contained in that simplicity. "A saint is someone who lets the light shine through."

Regardless of the definition applied, however, all Christendom certainly would agree that among the Church's great saints, a significant place belongs to Francis of Assisi. He was a gentle man who clearly served Christ with his whole being. By so doing, his radiant faith drew people to himself from all levels of society. He still draws people to the Christ he served, eight hundred years after his birth. What is there about this man that was (and is) so attractive? We might find many answers, but a common thread running through them all would be that he loved everyone and everything. He devoted himself to doing good for all people and for all of God's creatures, because he loved God so fully.

Francis was the kind of person who never withheld a kindness from a friend. He never withheld a kindness from anyone or anything. As a prisoner of war, when money arrived from his family to ransom him, he gave it to a friend who had no family to send money. So Francis chose to remain behind in prison. Truly, he let the light shine through.

So it can be with us. We who claim to love the world as God loves the world must be willing to do good to all people. In case that is too general, we must be ready to do good to our neighbors, our fellow workers, our enemies, and the passersby who cross our path every day.

We find it easy to profess love for all the world. But we need to recognize that such love is not an emotion. It is, and must always be, an active verb.

It may be generally easy to do good to those of our family. It may even be easy to do good to your neighbors, or to a stranger who passes your way. But what about an enemy? Can you do good for someone who would like to destroy you? Yet that is precisely what Jesus demands of us. He expects us to love our enemies. This is where the question of the quality of our commitment to God really shows up. If we fail here, we have not really learned the lesson Jesus taught. Even from the Cross, Jesus looked down and prayed for those who nailed Him there.

Those of us who follow Jesus must learn to demonstrate our relation to God by the way we treat everyone and everything around us. We can begin with our friends. But we must go beyond, far beyond. The path to sainthood is simple. It simply requires doing good in God's name, everywhere, all the time.

It is simple. But it's not easy.

Merciful God, we thank Thee that Thou dost love us but hast not confined Thy love to us. Help us to love all Thy people and to show our love for Thee by doing good to others. This we pray for Christ's sake. Amen.

chapter eight

The Tasks That Isolate

GOING FROM BAD TO WORSE

> If you have raced with men on foot,
> and they have wearied you,
> how will you compete with horses?
> And if in a safe land you fall down,
> how will you do in the jungle of the Jordan?
>
> *JEREMIAH 12:5*

Did you ever complain to God about your lot in life? Most of us have at one time or another. Jeremiah had just been going through such a time, when God responded with the words of our text.

Freely paraphrased, God was saying to His prophet, "If you have become exhausted in the footrace you've been in, what are you going to do in the horse race I've entered you in next? Remember, you won't even be riding a horse! And if you have tripped and fallen as you ran over the level ground, how will you stay on your feet when you have to run through the thicket of the Jordan Valley?" In other words, God was saying to Jeremiah, "Cheer up! The worst is yet to come!"

There has been a false idea going around that if a person becomes a Christian, everything is going to be all right. That just isn't so. God has never promised a life of ease and comfort to his people. The Bible clearly indicates that this is not true. Furthermore, the history of the Church's life plainly demonstrates that God's greatest saints did not have an easy time of it at all. In fact, the opposite is usually true. Becoming a Christian opens the door to ridicule, opposition, hostility, suffering, and sometimes even death. Yet the testimony of God's servants has consistently been that whatever comes, it is worth it. There are the moments when the humanity of God's suffering servants cries out in agony. But the evidence given at the end of life is universally of the opposite nature. Whatever may have come, it has been well worth it.

So do not expect flowery beds of ease if you put your feet on the Gospel road. Rather, you may expect things to go from bad to worse. Serving the God who loves you may isolate you from friends and family. Others may never understand what it is that has caught your imagination and captured your life. Tell them, simply, you have become the victim of a greater love.

God never calls us to a difficult way without first clearly pointing out the risks, the dangers, and the possible costs. He does not ask us to be blind servants. But He does call us to consider the difficulties and then bear the burdens of serving Him.

It is then that life suddenly takes on a new dimension. Present suffering will certainly be real. But that is never the whole story. There is always more beyond. God never leaves us alone in our difficulties. He is always with us. And through Jesus Christ, He has endured the same. God never calls us to go where He has not gone first. We are called to follow. We can do no more. We should do no less.

Merciful God, we cannot comprehend all the suffering of this present time, but we accept them as part of the life Thou hast called us to lead. Give us grace to follow Thy Son through the power of Thy Spirit. In Jesus' name we pray. Amen.

LIVING IN CRITICAL TIMES

And the word of the Lord came to me, saying, "Jeremiah, what do you see?" And I said, "I see a rod of almond." Then the Lord said to me,

"You have seen well, for I am watching over my word to perform it."

JEREMIAH 1:11-12

Have you ever lived through a major crisis, wondering where God was? Have you ever felt that God just did not care about what was happening in your life or in your world? Most of us have had such feelings at one time or another. At these times, life has come with such blows that we may have felt that God had abandoned us. What do you do at such times? Perhaps it is even more appropriate to ask, what can you do at such times? .

Jeremiah's ministry was lived in the catastrophic last days of Judah. It appeared that no one cared that the ultimate judgment of God was about to fall. In fact, Jeremiah was even wondering whether or not God cared. He was beset by two questions. First, did God really care? Second, was God going to keep His promises?

Jeremiah first of all took his difficult questions to God. He did not just give up on God, he actually asked God about it. Now that is the real nature of prayer. Even when, or especially when, we have doubts about God, we need to lay them honestly before Him. God is not threatened by our hostility or by our doubts. But Jeremiah did more than ask, he waited for God's answer. Looking and listening, Jeremiah believed that God would give him an answer to his dilemma.

He found his answer as he walked over his family farm one day. He had stopped to gaze at an almond tree, when God spoke to him. In the Hebrew language, the world for almond is *shaqed*. It literally means "awake." The tree is so named because it is the first tree to bloom in the spring in Palestine. Thus it was the first tree to awake. As Jeremiah looked at the "awake" tree, God told him that he was awake, watching over His Word. The word "watching" is *shoqed*, and is related to the first one. God revealed to His prophet that He was not asleep. He was aware of what was going on.

Now it is important to note that God neither rebuked Jeremiah for his doubt nor for his anxiety. Rather, He simply called upon the prophet to trust Him a little longer. What Jeremiah had thought was evidence that God did not care, was evidence instead that God cared very much. He cared so much about what was going on that He was being patient.

We must never mistake God's patience with a lack of caring. When we live through critical times, let us learn to trust in God's patience. Love is always patient. God does not forget His world.

If God had not been patient with those involved when Stephen was stoned, the Church would never have had a Paul. If Jesus had not been consistently patient with the weaknesses of Simon Peter, we would not have had his great sermon at Pentecost. Let us rejoice, then, that even in critical times, God is patient. He is patient with others. And, thank goodness, He is also patient with us.

O God of time and eternity, may we never become so engrossed in the moment that we forget that Thou hast all time in Thy hand. Help us to be patient in our critical times, even as Thou art. May Thy Holy Spirit give us patience with others and ourselves, for we ask it in Jesus' holy name. Amen.

ESTABLISHING PRIORITIES

And do you seek great things for yourself? Seek them not; for, behold, I am bringing evil upon all flesh, say the Lord; but I will give you your life as a prize of war in all places to which you may go.

JEREMIAH 45:5

There is nothing either good or evil in ambition. What matters is what we do with it or what we allow it to do with us. Baruch, Jeremiah's scribe, was obviously a highly trained man with great abilities and genuine courage. These showed up early in his service to Jeremiah.

He was also apparently highly ambitious. The problem with his ambition was that he had let it get out of proper perspective.

In the catastrophic days that were descending upon Judah, which Jeremiah had foretold, there were going to be matters of far more importance than merely achieving greatness. In fact, according to Jeremiah, mere survival was going to be the basic issue confronting his people.

It was against this background that God offered Baruch the promise that he would survive the Babylonian invasion. When viewed against the background of the great things Baruch wished to accomplish, mere survival may not have sounded like much. But, when viewed against the multitudes who were about to fall victim to the armies of Babylon, mere survival was quite important. For Baruch, it was a matter of putting his priorities in the right perspective.

In a very real sense, the same is true for us. The problem is that most of us never really see things as God sees them. We, like Baruch, may set our sights on greatness. That may not even be a matter of pride. Our ambition may be to accomplish great things for God. There is nothing wrong with that as long as it fits into God's plan. Sometimes we cannot achieve our ambitions and do what we have been called to do at the same time.

The point we must face again and again is that we are not and never have been necessarily called to greatness. We have been called to faithfulness. We must always face the issue of getting our priorities in line with those of God.

The cross on the steeple of a church is no greater in importance than the unseen spikes that hold the beams supporting that cross. But the cross is seen, while the spikes fulfill their purpose unseen. If they fail, however, the cross will fall.

The same is true of our place in God's kingdom. Most of us are called to serve unseen and unheralded. But that does not mean that we are less important in God's great plan. It may be that the ministry of God's unsung and unseen heroes and heroines is far more important than that of those whose fame is blazed across the skies.

Our priority must always be to accept that which God has planned for us. Only then can we really fulfill our purpose in His plan. We are called to faithfulness, not to greatness. But when all is said and done, faithfulness is the way of greatness.

Grant to us, O Lord, that we may know and understand what it is that Thou has planned for us. Give us the contentment to accept Thy will for our lives, neither envying others' places, nor abandoning our own. This we pray in the name of Thy Son, our Lord, who truly showed us the way of obedient faith. Amen.

CHANGING DIRECTIONS IN LIFE

Then Amos answered Amaziah, "I am no prophet, nor a prophet's son; but I am a herdsman, and a dresser of sycamore trees, and the Lord took me from following the flock, and the Lord said to me, 'Go, prophesy to my people Israel.'

"Now therefore hear the word of the Lord."

AMOS 7:14-16a

What is it that is important enough to cause a man to leave his life's vocation and set out on the thankless task of being a prophet to a people who do not want any word from God? What is it that is powerful enough to cause young people to leave a safe environment and go to the ends of the earth to be missionaries to people with a foreign language and an alien culture?

Ancient as well as modern history is filled with stories of those who have left everything behind in order to become a missionary, a prophet, or a preacher. They go to tell others about God, to share the good news that God loves them. But they also go to minister to the whole person, seeking to help them medically, intellectually, and in business and agriculture. They go, driven by some kind of inner compulsion that is hard to identify and harder still to describe. But they go, in a seemingly never ending train.

If such things happened only occasionally, it would be easy

to pass them off as some kind of mental or emotional aberration. But it happens far too frequently for that kind of glib explanation. It happens to youths on the threshhold of life, to successful, mature adults, and even to older adults in the very sunset days of life.

What is it, this drive that causes well-adjusted people to utterly change directions in life?

For the prophet Amos, the answer to this perplexing question was quite simple: "The Lord took me." Somehow, God invaded the life of Amos and showed him greater needs than leading a flock of sheep. He also showed him a more challenging task than pruning sycamore trees. So it was that he who had led sheep suddenly became a leader of people. This laborer who had cut off fruitless branches began to uproot fruitless lives.

We are not given the details of God's confrontation with Amos, such as we are given about some of the other prophets. But there is no doubt that it happened. Amos spoke of hearing God's voice like the roar of a lion. He reported having his whole life's patterns uprooted and redirected. We do not know much about Amos before his call. But we clearly see that after his call he fearlessly spoke of God in the city streets, the market places, and the religious shrines, confronting evil on the part of religious, political, and social leaders. He had no fear of the important, the powerful, or the wealthy. Rather, his only fear seems to have been that they would not heed his message. He sought to call the people to meet the God he had met.

God certainly transforms our lives. He calls us to a new direction, to a new task. Yet when He calls, He often uses the skills we have already developed. God never wastes anything. In following God's new direction, we can use the same gifts we have always had. How have you responded to the call of God?

Open our eyes and ears, O Lord, to the call of Thy Spirit, that we may be willing to leave behind that which has prepared us for the greater tasks to which Thou dost call. Give to us the motivation

*that will help us face Thy future fearlessly and faithfully. In Jesus'
name we pray. Amen.*

DESPISING GOD'S SERVANT

He was despised and rejected by men;
a man of sorrows, and acquainted with grief;
and as one from whom men hid their faces
he was despised, and we esteemed him not.

ISAIAH 53:3

Centuries before the birth of Jesus of Nazareth, one of God's
ancient spokesmen pointed to the kind of experience God's Suffering Servant would undergo. It is a fascinating picture. But, if we
can tear our minds away from this portrait of suffering for a moment, there is another dimension we need to consider. The question
"Why?" deserves an answer.

We view the experience of Jesus and this magnificent poem
from *this* side of the Cross. Our perspective obviously colors our
grasp of what happened. Yet, at the same time, as we consider the
life of Jesus, it is difficult to see what it was about Him that made
it necessary for His world to crucify Him. We read of His tenderness, His compassion, and His healing power, and wonder why
anyone would want to kill Him. We consider how He welcomed
outcasts, gave dignity to women, loved those whom no one else
cared for, and we cannot comprehend why there was a conspiracy
to remove Him from their midst. Of course, He was different from
most of the people of His day. In fact, He was different from all of
them. But that is not a sufficient reason to explain His betrayal,
arrest, trial, and execution.

No one has ever been so human, and at the same time been so
isolated from all His contemporaries. In the end, it was one of His
own followers who betrayed Him. Furthermore, not one of them

86

stood with Him during the hours of His trial. He was totally, utterly, and completely forsaken.

As we ponder the life and death of Jesus over and over again, we still can come to no explanation as to *why* He was killed. It just doesn't seem to make sense.

But before we turn away from the problem too quickly, let us consider first what we do with this same Jesus in our world. He is given lip service by thousands, but obedience by few. In a world that fears the power of the atom, yet that builds more and more of these weapons of ultimate destruction, He who spoke of peace is ignored.

Are we any less guilty than the people of the first century? Have we not just as thoroughly despised and rejected Him? Even those of us who claim to follow Him in total commitment find it difficult to get along with His expectations. The real tragedy of our day is not the atheism, the agnosticism, or the secularism; it is the tragedy of Christians who do not love one another. Have we not rejected His Lordship and despised His teachings? Do we find it any easier to obey Him than did our first-century neighbors?

It is easy to wonder how that happened to Jesus in the first century. But it really isn't difficult to believe that we would do the same thing to Him if He had come to us in this century. We still despise and reject those who fully serve God. God's service is still a task that isolates, and this is especially true of Jesus.

Forgive us, O Lord, for our failure to follow Thee and to obey Thee. We know our unworthiness, but we throw ourselves upon Thy mercy, begging for cleansing through Him who both died because of us and also for us. Help us to follow Christ fully, for it is in His name that we pray. Amen.

When the young Isaiah volunteered to become a prophet of the God who had cleansed him of sin, he was given what appeared to be a thankless, hopeless task. The prospect of this kind of ministry overwhelmed the eager new prophet. Out of his shock, he turned back to God, questioning.

> Then I said, "How long, O Lord?"
> And he said: "Until cities lie waste
> without inhabitant, and houses without men,
> and the land is utterly desolate."
> *ISAIAH 6:11*

The reality that the prophet had to face, but did not wish to, was that God had called him to be a magnificent failure! That is shocking.

Given the success-oriented mind frame of contemporary culture, you and I find this kind of experience both terrifying and unbelievable. Everybody expects to be a success. How can we fit into our thought processes the idea that we may be called to fail?

There is nothing inherently wrong with success. There are some people who seem to think that success is a sin. That is not what the Bible says at all. But the shocking point is that failure is no sin either.

God can be honored by a faithful failure just as much as by a faithful success. But He is more honored by a faithful servant who fails than He is by an unfaithful servant who succeeds. There is no place in the Christian Gospel for the idea that the end result is all that is important.

Somehow, our Christian view of life needs to be enlarged to make room for those who are called to fail. William Carey, founder of the modern missionary movement, labored for years without a single convert. All that time and effort were expended without one single outward result to show for it! By the world's standards, he was a failure. But God doesn't measure by those standards. His standards are different, quite different.

How do we deal with this, then?

Well, we first recognize that Jesus described the kingdom in terms of images such as leaven and salt, among other things. Both of these things work silently, invisibly, to accomplish their purpose. Not all ministry produces results that can be seen.

Next, we must note that God's ways are not our ways. His purposes may be different from ours. We cannot judge His accomplishments by our standards. It is rather ridiculous for us, then, to pass judgment on His faithful servants. We will know the whole truth by and by. Only He knows it now.

Finally, it is in our weakness and failure that God most clearly demonstrates His power. If the kingdom came in upon a series of human successes, we could, and probably would, take the credit for our accomplishments. The fact that God brings His kingdom through our failures removes all basis for personal pride.

Let us, then, not be so quick to judge failure. Let us rather look for faithfulness. It is that to which God calls us. It is that for which He looks. And it is that which He will use to effect His will on earth through His human servants.

Grant to us, dear God, that we may not measure either our or others' faithfulness by standards of success. Help us, rather, to be obedient to Thy call, being willing to be isolated from the so-called normal patterns of life. This we pray through Jesus Christ, our Lord. Amen.

chapter nine

The Sin That Alienates

DIVORCING ONESELF FROM GOD

> Create in me a clean heart, O God,
> and put a new and right spirit within me.
> Cast me not away from thy presence,
> and take not thy holy Spirit from me.
>
> *PSALM 51:10-11*

If there is any Biblical teaching you and I have fully tested through practical experience, it is that, when we do wrong, we separate ourselves from God. This harsh fact of reality is the inescapable consequence of traveling a path of sinful rebellion. No matter what excuses we may offer, no matter in what terms we may express it, our sin divorces us from a loving relationship with the Father.

The psalmist, crying out from the innermost part of his being, agonized over the fact that his sin had separated him from the presence of God's Spirit.

Sin isolates. We have talked about how God's holiness cannot abide the presence of sin. But the fact that almost always catches us by surprise is that our sin first causes us to flee from God's presence. The ultimate divorce process is begun by our flight into infidelity.

It is true that sin isolates us from God. It also isolates us from all that is good. We drive barriers between ourselves and others. The overwhelming awareness of the guilty sinner is that of aloneness. We may try to cover this up by a frantic social pace and by eager activity. But in those still, dark moments of the night, we know that we are alone. In our guilt, every relation becomes superficial. The more eagerly we pursue the companionship of superficial friends, the more clearly we are aware of just how isolated our lives have become.

The utter aloneness is a tragedy.

Ultimately, in our aloneness, we realize that though we have separated ourselves from God, He still loves us. Even His judgment on our sin is a testimony that He cares. It is when we realize this that we are ready to turn back to Him for forgiveness and restoration.

Again, the psalmist tutors us. He knew that the only way for the divorce to be healed was by the creation of a clean heart within. He needed a new spirit of righteousness to guide him. There are places where we can go to get dirty clothes cleaned. There are places where we can go to get dirty rugs, drapes, and upholstery cleaned. But if anyone could find a way to get dirty lives cleaned up, almost any price could be charged.

Yet, that is precisely what God is about. In Christ Jesus, He is in the business of making dirty lives clean. He who created us in the first place, can create a clean heart and a new and right spirit for us.

It is true, then, that sin isolates, divorcing us from a loving relationship with God. But it *never* divorces us from God's love. So He takes the hurt into Himself, offering us a new relationship through His forgiveness. Our sinful divorce can be healed. Now that is good news.

O God, Thou who hast loved us and given Thyself for us, help us to turn from our alienating sin, accepting Thy love and forgiveness, and living in a new and loving relationship with Thee. This we pray through the name of Him who came to cleanse us from every sin, even Jesus our Lord. Amen.

And Jonathan spoke well of David to Saul his Father, and said to him, "Let not the king sin against his servant David; because he has not sinned against you, and because his deeds have been of good service to you; for he took his life in his hand and he slew the Philistine, and the Lord wrought a great victory for all Israel. You saw it, and rejoiced; why then will you sin against innocent blood by killing David without cause?"

1 SAMUEL 19:4-5

We find it easy to believe that sin isolates us from God. That does not really seem to surprise anyone. But we find it a bit more difficult to accept (until we experience the fact) that sin causes us to be isolated from our friends. Human relationships are just as thoroughly destroyed by our sin as the divine relationship.

Over and over again in my ministry, as I counseled people with marital difficulties, I have heard statements like the following from angry and distraught spouses: "She's just not the same woman I married!" "He's just not the same person he used to be!" Of course they are the same persons! No one has come along and changed partners on them.

What has gone wrong in many cases is that sin has entered into one life or the other and has alienated them from each other. Sin in our hearts and lives causes us to reject those who love us, for their presence awakens our conscience, stabbing our hearts with guilt. It is this that causes us to try to cover it up by isolating ourselves from both family and friends. Sin is truly isolating.

Jonathan lovingly rebuked his father's rejection of their friend David, pointing out that the problem was not David's, but Saul's. The king had to be made to face the fact that the course of action he was following against David was the way of sin. He had isolated himself from David by his own sin.

This is a fact of life we all need to face. When our loving relationships begin to disintegrate, we need first of all to examine ourselves, seeing if the sin separating us is our own. More often than not, it will be.

When we begin to discover that our friendships and our family ties are beginning to be strained, the first step we must take is that of confessing our own sin and begging for forgiveness. If we are going to truly show the world what God can do with our sin, we must begin by showing that we can and do want to maintain our relationships. Sin must never be allowed to get a toehold in our communities of love. Furthermore, we also need to be able to warn others when we become aware that their sin is destroying their relationships with others. This must be done with gentle love, but it must be done. Ignoring the problem will not solve it. It will only grow worse. We must learn to maintain our relationships by confessing our sin, and by forgiving others their sin.

Help us, O Lord, that we may not allow sin to separate us from our loved ones, that we may confess any sin that has isolated us, and that we may both forgive and find forgiveness for such sin. In Jesus' name we pray. Amen.

LEAVING GOD BEHIND

Mention the name Samson, and people immediately think of an ancient strong man who wasted a large part of his strength in sexual license. From his early adulthood, Samson appears to have had a weakness for women. Ultimately, his weakness led him to the Philistine temptress, Delilah. She was a pawn in the hands of the Philistine lords, who sought to use her to destroy Samson. Finally, she seduced him into revealing the source of his great strength, thus discovering his Nazirite vow.

> She made him sleep upon her knees; and she called a man, and had him shave off the seven locks of his head. Then she began to torment

him and his strength left him. And she said, "The Philistines are upon you, Samson!" And he awoke from his sleep, and said, "I will go out as at other times, and shake myself free." And he did not know that the Lord had left him.

JUDGES 16:19-20

The tragedy of Samson's life was that he had assumed that since God had always been with him, God would always be with him. He never realized that when he was playing around with sin, he was also playing around with God's presence in his life.

We usually make the assumption that God will always be there when we need Him. That is certainly false. God is not some kind of celestial bellhop who is always ready to come when we call.

Furthermore, another aspect of Samson's tragic story is even more frightening. When he awoke from his sleep, he did not even know that God had departed from him. Samson had left God behind as he traveled down the path of sin. But he assumed that God would never leave him behind. He was wrong.

So are we, if we assume that God will not abandon us to our sin. To the prophets of the Old Testament, the ultimate punishment of those who abandoned God was that God simply let them go. He no longer struggled with the perverse, rebellious sinner. He still doesn't. God's grace keeps seeking to draw us back to Him as we begin traveling on the path of sin. But if we persist, somewhere along the way God allows us to go on, alone.

Sin, in its beginning, is to forsake God. In its end, it is to be God forsaken.

The sad, short story of any one of us who begins to turn away from God is that we may not be the only one who turns. God also may turn from us. Furthermore, our turning away is all the more tragic because we have once known both His love and His grace. Having shared the loving fellowship of God and then to abandon Him is the utmost folly. But it is precisely our foolishness that leads us to travel such a path, to perform such an act.

It is up to us, then, to determine that the path of our lives shall not be directed away from God. Rather, we should cling to Him as He holds to us. The love of God will hold on to us as long as we wish to be in fellowship with Him. But we cannot hold on to both God and sin. One must be abandoned. We must choose God consciously. It cannot be any other way. To choose sin is ultimately to leave God behind.

God of mercy, help us to experience Thy mercy in its fulness, not presuming upon it in our arrogance. Grant to us that we may not turn away from Thy love to follow our own path into sin. This we pray through Him who showed us the way. Amen.

EMPTYING RITUAL OF MEANING

I hate, I despise your feasts,
and I take no delight in your solemn assemblies.
Even though you offer me your burnt offerings
and cereal offerings, I will not accept them,
and the peace offerings of your fatted beasts
I will not look upon.
Take away from me the noise of your songs;
to the melody of your harps I will not listen.
But let justice roll down like waters,
and righteousness like an ever-flowing stream.

AMOS 5:21-24

Religious rituals receive a very mixed reaction from Christians and non-Christians alike. Some people hardly believe that they can worship without an elaborate ritual, while others see rituals as some kind of mumbojumbo that is wholly devoid of meaning. To the ancient Hebrews, ritual was a basic way of drawing near to God, without offending His holiness. It set up both the means and the manner of humanity's approach to the God who saved.

Unfortunately, the ritual of Israelite worship suffered significant abuse. In fact, anything, no matter how good, can be prostituted to become evil. The prophet Amos leveled a devastating attack upon his people who viewed ritual as the only important thing in their relationship to God. They had been scrupulous in observing the ritual, and totally unscrupulous in their treatment of other people. By practicing proper ritual and unrighteousness at the same time, they had wholly emptied their ritual of any meaning. They had also emptied it of any effectiveness. Proper ritual performed by an unrighteous worshipper was totally rejected by God. This was a surprising truth to ancient Israel. It is still a surprising truth to contemporary Christians. It is of no significance how we worship if we are guilty of not practicing the practicalities of dealing justly with all people.

The finest choirs, the greatest music, the most outstanding sermons, and the most beautiful sanctuaries are utterly worthless if we have not first demonstrated our faith in daily living. Now this does not mean that sinful people should not come to worship. If that were true, there would be no one who worshipped. But it clearly means that unrepentant sinners cannot fully approach God in worship. Our offerings, anthems, rituals, and proclamations become wholly empty if they are built upon a week of ill-gotten gain and cruel oppression of our neighbors.

The sad, tragic truth is that all too frequently our sin has so alienated us from God, that our ritual cannot bridge the gap. We who serve God in Christ, must first learn to do so in the marketplace before we can do so in the sanctuary. We must allow justice and righteousness to flow through our lives seven days a week before we draw near to God at our times of worship. Practical righteousness must precede proper worship in our service of God.

O God, Thou hast called us to approach Thee in worship, and we would come through Christ Jesus. Yet, we need Thy help in order to practice righteousness toward others, so that we can be prepar-

ed for worship. Grant us the courage and the purpose to treat others with justice, so that we may worship Thee fully. This we pray in Jesus' name. Amen.

DESTROYING RELATIONSHIPS

Cain said to Abel his brother, "Let us go out to the field." And when they were in the field, Cain rose up against his brother Abel, and killed him. Then the Lord said to Cain, "Where is Abel your brother?" He said, "I do not know; am I my brother's keeper?" And the Lord said, "What have you done? The voice of your brother's blood is crying to me from the ground."

GENESIS 4:8-10

The first murder obviously sprang from sin. For Cain, it was an attempt to alleviate an unhappy situation. He was unhappy with his brother, Abel, because Abel's service to God had been better than his own. Cain could have sought to become a better servant of God, but he chose another way. Rather than get more involved with God, he decided to eliminate Abel. What a foolish course of action!

Yet that is precisely the course of action many of us take in similar situations. Now I do not mean that we go out and murder someone. What we do is something less obvious, but more insidious than that. We note someone who seems to be a better, more faithful servant of God than we, and so we begin to attack them verbally. We impugn their motives for service. Or perhaps we pass on some malicious gossip, implying untruths that we might not actually speak. It may be that we begin to search for some flaw in their character, which we can then attack with glee. The end result is clearly the same. As far as the world is concerned, we have destroyed someone else's effective service of God.

Cain's sin had destroyed his relationship long before he rose up to slay his brother. Then, when God sought to confront his sin, Cain self-righteously protested that he was not his brother's keeper. He was clearly wrong. His sin had blinded him to his responsibility for his brother.

In the centuries that have passed, those of us who have followed Jesus Christ have been made quite aware that we *are* our brothers' keepers. We *are* responsible. But there is more. Jesus' teachings have led us to an even more demanding responsibility. It is obvious from Genesis that I am my brother's or my sister's keeper. That is not debatable.

But Jesus teaches that, more than being a keeper, I am also my brother's brother. However, even that is not the full truth. He also says that I am to be the stranger's brother. I must take in the stranger, offering love and welcome. But even this is not the end of Christ's demands.

Jesus also teaches that I am my enemy's brother. I must love and do good to those who would persecute and destroy me. That is the way Jesus lived. And that is the way He calls us to live.

Anything less than this in my life is sin. The relationships to which God has called me are destroyed by my sin at any point in this list where I fail. I do not have to kill to destroy these relationships. I simply have to fail to do good for my brother, for the stranger, or for my enemy. At that point, my sin has destroyed my relationship with God's people. Ultimately, it has destroyed my relationship with God.

Merciful God, we thank Thee that Thou hast loved us while we were yet sinners, alienated from Thee. Help us to love Thy people, no matter what their attitude toward us. Give us the grace to do deeds of loving kindness, even to those who do not want them. This we pray through Him who set us the example, even Jesus our Lord. Amen.

It is easy to stand in judgment upon God. When King Uzziah died, Isaiah went into the temple, apparently seeking to call God to account for the way Uzziah had been treated. He had been a relatively good king. Yet he had been forced to live the latter part of his life as a leper, finally dying as an outcast. Isaiah wanted to know what kind of God would have so abused this good king. In the temple, however, Isaiah had a vision of God, discovering that God is holy. Both Uzziah and Isaiah had taken God too lightly. We dare not ignore the awesome holiness of God. When Isaiah discovered this aspect of God's nature, he suddenly saw himself as he was. It was then that he cried,

> Woe is me! For I am lost; for I am a man of unclean lips, and I dwell in the midst of a people of unclean lips; for my eyes have seen the King, the Lord of hosts!
>
> *ISAIAH 6:5*

We, like Isaiah, frequently approach God from the standpoint of our pride. We are so sure that we have a fully developed sense of justice and righteousness. We also feel that we know just how someone ought to deal with this world from a position of mercy and love. The basic thing we fail to face is that our knowledge is limited, our experience is limited, our wisdom is limited, and our judgment is certainly limited.

Thus, to try to call God to account is a matter of arrogant pride. It is at this point that we should face the fact—although we often don't—that pride is sin. Instead of approaching God to listen, or even to converse, we have approached Him from the standpoint of our own sin.

Isaiah discovered that he was not on equal footing with God, he was utterly alone. His sinful, arrogant words had isolated him from God. It was his sense of utter aloneness that so overwhelmed him.

There are many people who reject the mental image of God

that they have picked up. It may have come through seeing weak Christians. It may have come through reading. It may even have come through their own inner reflections. But the point is, the God they have rejected is not the God of the Bible. It is merely a twisted, distorted image of Him. When Isaiah grasped the real nature of God, he was no longer standing before Him demanding an answer. He was suddenly prostrate before Him, begging forgiveness.

As soon as we really grasp the fulness of God's nature, then we are in a position to see ourselves as we are. Then we are aware that it is our own sin that has isolated us from God. It is not that we have rejected Him, but that we have never known Him. We have rejected our own distortions of Him.

This is what our sinful pride does to us. It causes us to have spiritual astigmatism. Seeing God, however, brings us to the place where we realize how alone we are in our sin and how much we need the presence and the cleansing, forgiving power of God. Then we can see not merely how alone we are, but also how God does not wish us to be that way. We become aware that He does come to us, even when we have isolated ourselves from Him. That is the good news of Jesus Christ. He is God come in human flesh to deliver us from our sinful aloneness. That is good news. We dare to believe it. We rejoice to tell it.

Gratefully, O Lord, we come to Thee, rejoicing in the fact that Thou hast not left us alone in our sins. We are thankful that Thou hast delivered us from that isolation into the full love of Thy presence by the redemption of Jesus Christ, in whose name we pray. Amen.

chapter ten

The Guilt That Oppresses

DEVASTATED BY GUILT

Cain said to the Lord,
"My punishment is greater than I can bear."
GENESIS 4:13

When you and I are first brought up short by being confronted with our sin and our sinful nature, we frequently cry out within our hearts something similar to these words of Cain. We are horrified at the punishment our sin brings. It always begins with alienation from family and friends. It may even involve the breaking of a marriage or the shattering of a family. It may involve other temporal consequences as well. And, of course, there is our alienation from God, which is also a part of the punishment. By our sin, we have erected a barrier between ourselves and a loving fellowship with God. Truly, we can identify with the heart-rending cry, "My punishment is greater than I can bear." Our very souls shudder at that agonizing confession.

But there is an even deeper message here. The Hebrew word translated "punishment" also means "guilt." Thus, Cain may have been crying out not merely at his punishment, but at the burden of guilt he was bearing. It is imperative that you and I recognize that the real burden we bear is that of guilt, not merely of punishment. Far too much of our lives is involved with frustration or despondency at the prospect of our punishment. It almost appears as if we have created an eleventh commandment, "Thou shalt not get caught." Agony over our punishment for sin may lead to remorse. It seldom leads to repentance and restoration. Remorse is a spiritual dead end. It leads nowhere.

On the other hand, when our spiritual sensitivities are aroused enough for us to become aware of the burden of guilt we bear, then we are at least conscious of a need for correction. I can avoid the burden of punishment by not being caught. I can only avoid the burden of guilt by not being guilty.

Yet this brings us face to face with a new dilemma. When we are guilty of sin and rebellion, there is nothing we can do to remove our guilt. The greatest agony of guilt is that it can never be escaped. When we are guilty, we are never able to avoid the presence of guilt. If this were the whole story, we would be facing an absolute pit of despondency and despair.

But God is also aware of this dilemma. So He, in His love and mercy, has provided an escape from the burden of guilt through Jesus Christ. This is proclaimed in two ways. First of all, God as righteous Judge offers us pardon through His grace by faith in Jesus. Yet, even pardon does not remove guilt. It just eliminates the consequences. So we are also offered new life. We are made new creatures in Christ Jesus by our faith. This is one of the joys of being "born again." Now, by God's grace, we have been recreated. Our guilt is gone. Thus God can do more with sin than forgive it. He can remove the guilt it causes. When that is done by His love, we stand with the burden lifted. The utter devastation of guilt is gone.

The burden of guilt is always greater than we can bear, but it is never greater than God can bear. And so He does, in Christ.

O God of mercy, we rejoice that Thou hast made it possible through Jesus Christ that the burden of our guilt can be removed. We accept our new innocence before Thee. Help us to be eager to share this message with others who bear the burden of guilt. This we pray through Jesus Christ. Amen.

CONDEMNING THE UNFAITHFUL

Hear the word of the Lord, O people of Israel;
for the Lord has a controversy with the inhabitants
of the land. There is no faithfulness or kindness,
and no knowledge of God in the land;
there is swearing, lying, killing, stealing,
and committing adultery;
they break all bounds and murder follows murder.

HOSEA 4:1-2

Your sin and mine is never winked at by God. There are times when we mistake God's patience with us for an indication that He just doesn't care. That is wholly wrong. We must be careful not to confuse His patience with indifference.

We should be grateful for His patience. An impatient Lord would have gotten rid of you and me long ago. If God's entire concern were simply to have a sinless world, He could have accomplished that easily by getting rid of mankind. But God has other concerns. Among His prime concerns is having a righteous people. It is not merely enough not to do wrong; God desires us to be good.

The attack of Hosea is quite specific at this point. The Hebrew word translated "no" in our passage is more than a simple negative. Rather, this word refers to the absence of something that ought to be present. When we see an airplane, we expect it to have wings and a tail. Yet, I passed a truck on the highway the other day that was transporting a dismantled airplane. Both the wings and the tail had been removed. Quite literally, I saw a plane "with an absence of wings and tail." I had every right to expect these features to be present, but they weren't. So it was with Hosea's denunciation of his unfaithful people. There was an absence of faithfulness, kindness, and experience with God. These were the people of God and those characteristics should have been present.

It was because the positive aspects of their relationship with

God were missing, that the obvious sins of disobedience crept in, or swept in. It is quite simple, really. The life that is not filled with doing the things that please God, will certainly be filled with doing those that displease Him.

Once you and I turn away from God, then we immediately begin to fill our lives with evil. It is intriguing to note the difference between Hosea's charges and those that we moderns frequently make. We usually begin by attacking the evil. Hosea began by pointing out the absence of good. Furthermore, if any solution is going to be found to our problem, it is going to have to be done by meeting both sets of needs. We must turn away from our evil deeds. But that alone is not enough. We must also seek God's presence, do His will, follow His purposes. Then we shall be filling our lives with those things that God has every right to expect of His people. Of course, the first step to these things is through God's Son, Jesus. It is He who makes it possible for us to enter into an experiential relationship with God. And it is this relationship which then allows us to become characterized by both faithfulness and kindness.

Gracious God, help us to face the fulness of the sin within our lives, not merely by turning away from evil, but by turning to Thee in love and trust, finding it possible to do Thy will. This we pray in the name of Him who showed us how, even Jesus Christ, Thy Son, our Lord. Amen.

PRESSED DOWN BY SIN

There is no soundness in my flesh
because of thy indignation;
there is no health in my bones
because of my sin.

> For my iniquities have gone over my head;
> they weigh like a burden too heavy for me.
>
> *PSALM 38:3-4*

Have you ever stepped into quicksand? Suddenly, there is just nothing solid under your feet. Slowly, you begin to sink into what feels like slick goo with no bottom. As soon as you discover that you can get no solid footing, you begin to struggle to get out. Unfortunately, the more you struggle, the quicker you sink. Even your very clothes, as they get wet, become a weight that presses you more quickly into the muck. Everything you have carried becomes an excessive burden. If there is not someone around to pull you out, you will ultimately sink into the quicksand, disappearing from view, and from life. There won't even be a mark left to signify where you sank.

How like that is our experience with sin. Life seems to be moving along quite smoothly. No one but you knows what sins you are committing. And you find it quite easy to excuse them. Every sin seems justified at the moment you commit it. Then, one day, God comes on the scene. Suddenly you become aware of the fact that you are unworthy of Him. Your sin weighs you down, and you discover that your life has no foundations. Now you are quite aware that your sins are closing in on you. At one and the same time, your own guilt has removed the foundation from beneath your feet; it presses you down, and it sweeps over you until you are spiritually drowning in a sea of your own creation. You are also aware that there is no way you can rescue yourself from the morass of sin into which you are sinking.

Then you discover that you desperately need deliverance, yet no one seems to care. This is the ultimate feeling of being pressed down by sin. But this doesn't have to be the ultimate end.

For, in spite of the fact that you do not know it, *God cares for you.* He is not pleased with the guilt that drives you down into the bottomless pit you have dug for yourself. In spite of your iniquity, God loves you. Therefore, the fact that you are sinking in sin becomes the instrument of God's mercy, awakening you to the reality that you are being pressed down and cannot deliver yourself.

It is at this point that you are ready to hear that God loves you and that He has come to deliver you from the morass of guilt into which your sin is pressing you. It is not His will that you should perish. Rather, it is His will that you turn to Him for deliverance. He will lift you from the slough into which you are sinking. And he will also remove the sin that is pressing you down as well as sweeping over you. Furthermore, He will plant your spiritual feet upon the solid ground of His own being. However, sin will totally overwhelm you, pressing you down into despair and destruction, unless you turn to Him in faith. Thus, the end of the story does not have to be the despair of sin. It can be the mercy of God, which delivers from sin.

O Thou God of mercy, deliver us from the sin that presses us down and into which we sink. Take us from the bottomless pit of a meaningless existence, planting our feet on the path of righteousness. In Jesus' name we pray. Amen.

SURROUNDED BY SIN

For I know my transgressions,
and my sin is ever before me.
Against thee, thee only, have I sinned,
and done that which is evil in thy sight,
so that thou art justified in thy sentence
and blameless in thy judgment.

PSALM 51:3-4

Have you ever dreamed that you were trapped in a maze from which you could not escape or perhaps were enclosed in a room that had no door? If you haven't had either of these particular nightmares, you have surely had one like them. At one time or another, even those of us who are not victims of claustrophobia may have been haunted by a fear of being in some circumstance from which we could find no escape. This is a fairly common fear in human experience.

But the nightmare becomes a horrible reality when we find ourselves in a real situation from which there is no escape. This is the harsh reality of our sinfulness. In our text, the psalmist is crying out in anguish from the horror of being inescapably surrounded by sin.

Before doing a sinful act, we are able to deceive ourselves that it isn't so bad. But this is false. The first act of sin alienates us from God. It makes the second act easier to perform and less necessary to justify. Until, suddenly, we find ourselves enclosed by our own sense of sinfulness, from which there is no escape.

All the good works in the world cannot free me from my sense of guilt, nor from my awareness of being alienated from God. Suddenly I am alone, and there is no one who seems to care, no one who seems to be able to help. That is the tragic consequence of rebellion against God.

At the same time, no matter how I may have hurt others, or alienated myself from friends and family, I am most overwhelmed by the fact that my sin has ultimately been against God. However, this does not lessen the effects of sin on my relationships with others.

Furthermore, my guilt also makes me aware of my sin against myself. I have settled for less than I could have been. I cannot escape from my own sense of guilt. My guilt closes in on me, and there is nothing I can do. My sin encloses me, isolates me, and presses in on me. Try as I might, I can find no way out.

But there *is* a way out. While I cannot free myself from the enclosing tentacles of my sin, God can. Furthermore, He has already done so in Christ Jesus. He frees me from the inescapable, delivering me from the guilt that has surrounded and isolated me. This He does out of His abundant grace, only asking that I trust Him to forgive me. It is through His forgiveness, and only through His forgiveness, that I can find real freedom from guilt and sin.

O Thou God of mercy, we thank Thee that Thou hast come to us in Christ Jesus, offering forgiveness for our guilt, and freedom from the sin that enslaves us. Help us to cease our struggle to escape from our sin, trusting Thee for Thy deliverance. This we pray through the Spirit of Him who shattered the barriers of sin between us and Thee. Amen.

FAINTING FROM SIN

Why will you still be smitten,
that you continue to rebel?
The whole head is sick, and the whole heart faint.
From the sole of the foot
even to the head, there is no soundness in it,
but bruises and sores and bleeding wounds;
they are not pressed out, or bound up,
or softened with oil.

ISAIAH 1:5-6

There are occasions when the television or the newspaper carry pictures of an accident in which people are wounded so seriously and their condition is portrayed so vividly that it almost turns our stomachs. If someone tried to depict on television the utter horror of the images used by Isaiah to describe the conditions of his people, it would have the same effect. Israel was, quite literally, fainting from the consequences of her sinfulness. The judgments had come upon the people in ever increasing intensity, so that they were utterly devastated. The prophet was trying to get their attention by showing them in graphic detail the consequences of their rebellions: Sin and its consequent judgment should have driven them to the turning point—the "stomach-turning" point.

Two things stand out with clarity in Isaiah's proclamation. First, God's judgment had descended on the people of Israel not merely to punish them for their sin, but to try to get them to turn back to God from their sinfulness. The Old Testament prophets were quite certain that God's judgment in time was not simply penal. In fact, they were sure that it was primarily redemptive in purpose. The temporal consequences of sin were (and are) intended to drive us back to God for deliverance. Surely, sinful rebellion deserves and receives punishment. But God wants to forgive His people, and so He seeks to lead them to repentance. But this is not the whole story, nor even most of it.

Isaiah's second major truth was that Israel had stubbornly refused to turn back to God. They simply did not respond to the judgments as God had intended. One of the strange things about you and me is how often we get utterly stubborn about our plans for our own lives. We decide that our will is better than God's, that we know what is best for our lives, and that we will not turn from what we are doing. Though the load gets heavy and appears about to destroy us, we are still able to deceive ourselves into believing that if we can just hold on a little longer, things will improve. So we persistently follow our own paths, never becoming aware that we are separating ourselves further and further from God.

Over and over again, the prophets describe sin in terms of stubbornness. Perhaps we need to learn this lesson. The way of stubbornness is the way of utter separation from God and finally our destruction. If we are to survive spiritually, we must do so by turning to God from our sin, allowing Him to restore and heal us. There is no other way.

Merciful Father, we have stubbornly and selfishly sought our own way, planted our own seed; now we are reaping our own harvest. Help us, O Lord, that we may turn from our sin in repentance, finding both forgiveness and spiritual healing from Thee. Through Jesus Christ, Thy Son, our Lord, we pray. Amen.

Have mercy on me, O God, according to thy
stedfast love; according to thy abundant mercy
blot out my transgressions.
Wash me thoroughly from my iniquity,
and cleanse me from my sin!

PSALM 51:1-2

Ultimately, you and I always discover that the only thing we can really do with sin is to confess it to God, throwing ourselves upon His mercy in repentance. Our sin oppresses and destroys us if we do not bring it to God. Only he can forgive our sin. And only He can cleanse us of sin's consequences.

But this discovery is not always something new to us. It was not even new to the early Christians as they discovered that Jesus could and did deliver them from their own sinful natures. These hardy souls did discover *how* God forgave them, but there were saints more ancient than they who had *known* that God forgives. The prophets and the sweet singers of Israel had already known that God forgives sin. They had also known that only God can forgive sin. It did remain for Jesus to fully show in His own life and death how God accomplished His work of forgiveness.

Based upon the assurance that God forgives sin, the psalmist turned to God with his plea for forgiveness. To him, there were three steps to the ultimate, final cleansing of sin from the human heart.

First of all, the psalmist begged that his sin be blotted out. He was quite aware that sin had stained his life. He needed that stain to be blotted out, so that it would not be visible. In a sense, what he was asking for is what is accomplished when you erase something from a chalkboard. It is cleansed so that the old marks on it are not immediately visible.

But if you get up close to the chalkboard, or to our lives, you discover that mere blotting out is not enough. The old marks or stains are still visible to the close examination. There is more that needs to be done. Thus the psalmist pleaded that he be washed from his sin. Blotting got rid of the major evidence of sin. But there needs to be a more thorough removal of the marks. In a sense, this is *washing* the board to get rid of the remaining traces of chalk.

Yet, even this was not enough for the psalmist. For a very thorough, painstaking investigation would still find traces of the chalk, or the stain of sin. Thus there needs to be an absolute cleansing of the board, or of our lives, so that every trace of the old marks is gone. We might point up the progressive stages of cleansing for which the psalmist longed with this paraphrase:

"Blot out my sin, so that others cannot see it."
"Wash me from my sin, so that I cannot see it."
"Cleanse me thoroughly from my sin, so that You cannot see it."

Only God can cleanse sin this way; so thoroughly that even He cannot see it. This is the only way out from the tragic burden of sin. Let us rejoice that there is this way out.

We thank Thee, O Lord, that Thou hast not left us in our sin, but hast come to deliver us from our sin. In repentance we turn to Thee, throwing ourselves on Thy mercy, through Jesus Christ, Thy Son, our Lord, for it is in His name that we pray. Amen.

chapter eleven

The God Who Rescues

DELIVERING THE CAPTIVES

For the Lord has ransomed Jacob,
and redeemed him from hands too strong for him.
JEREMIAH 31:11

Many of us grew up on stories of knights in shining armor, who came riding up on white chargers to rescue princesses from evil captors. It did not take us long to discover that this was the stuff of fairy tales. In real life there just weren't any knights to rescue us from the troubles in which we found ourselves. This is tragic, for most of us feel that there ought to be, since life has so many problems.

The greatest problem in which we find ourselves and from which we need to be rescued is the problem of guilt. When we find ourselves sinking into sin, we struggle for release and find that we are powerless to overcome our own sin problem.

Yet this is precisely where our text suggests that God comes on the scene. It was not His pleasure to see His people suffering because of their sin. Even when His righteousness demanded that the sin be punished, yet His love still agonized with them in their punishment. The same is true today. God did not just suffer for sin in Christ Jesus. He suffers for our sin throughout all time. Just as the rings of a tree run from the bottom to the top, but are only visible where we cut into the trunk, so God's suffering for our sin runs throughout all eternity. But it was most visible at the Cross.

Yet God does more than suffer for our sin, He rescues us from our own suffering. The word translated "ransom" in our text has more of an emphasis on "rescue." There is no idea here of God paying anyone off. What He did for Israel, and what He does for us, is to break into history, delivering us from the consequences of our sin.

Surely, the most beautiful image of God found in the Old Testament is that of Him coming to deliver His people. When Israel was enslaved in Egypt, God delivered them. When they were in exile in Babylon, God delivered them. It was but a step from this for them to discover that when they were enslaved to sin, God would rescue. This is the kind of God He is.

God is never content to see His people held captive by sin. So His love seeks us out, offering us a way home with Him.

But, and this is important, though God delivers us, He never forces His deliverance upon us. Israel could have refused to leave Egypt. They could also have refused to leave Babylon. In fact, many of them did. And you and I can refuse to accept His deliverance. This we do by failing to accept His gift of forgiveness and life. The act of deliverance is always God's. But the choice to accept or reject is yours and mine.

The God who rescues will rescue, but He does not capture us. He allows us the choice. The wonder of His love is that He chooses to rescue at all, for we are unworthy and unlovely. His offer of deliverance is pure grace. He delivers us from what we deserve, offering us what we do not deserve—life with Him!

Dear God, we tremble in awe at the wonder of Thy love, which comes seeking us while we are yet in our sin. Help us to follow Thee from our sin into Thy love and forgiveness. This we pray through Thy Son, our Lord, Jesus Christ. Amen.

"I gave you cleanness of teeth in all your cities,
and lack of bread in all your places,
yet you did not return to me,"
says the Lord. . . .

"I overthrew some of you,
as when God overthrew Sodom and Gomorrah,
and you were as a brand plucked out of the burning;
yet you did not return to me,"
says the Lord.

AMOS 4:6, 11

Tragedy strikes, a crisis comes, and we cry out in grief, "Why did God do this to me?" The cry is both normal and natural. But we need to probe a bit deeper for the answer.

First of all, the Bible nowhere indicates that all tragedies or all crises come from God. Most come from the natural consequences of living in the world as it is. When a drunken driver runs down your loved ones, there is no way that the experience can be blamed on God. Furthermore, hurricanes and tornados are a natural part of life. Their immediate consequences cannot be blamed on God, as such.

On the other hand, the Old Testament is quite clear that God can and does use natural and historical events as the agents of His judgment. Isaiah viewed the Assyrian onslaught as an agent of God's judgment upon the sin of his people. Jeremiah saw the victorious armies of Babylon as God's instrument by which He punished Judah for their sinful rebellion. So it is quite clear that such events are used by God to judge the sin of His people.

But this brings up another question. What is God trying to accomplish by such acts of temporal judgment? The easy and obvious answer is that God is punishing sin. That may be quite true. His righteousness demands that sin be punished. But that is not the whole answer. In fact, it is not even most of the answer.

Amos clearly reflects the concept that God expected Israel

to turn to Him in repentance when the judgments fell. In fact, God was obviously disappointed when they did not. But the emphasis is that, to God, those temporal judgments were redemptive in purpose. They were intended to bring sinful people to their right senses, causing them to turn from their rebellious ways and to turn to God in obedient faithfulness.

God never delights in punishing sinful humanity. But he does it for our own good. The purpose behind His judgment is to get our attention, so that we will enter into a new fellowship with Him. God has no pleasure in our pain. His delight is in our obedience, for then we find real life at its fullest.

O Thou who sendest judgment upon us because of our sinfulness, help us to profit from that judgment by turning away from our stubborn rebellion and returning to Thee for mercy and renewed fellowship. Help us, also, to lead others to profit from Thy judgments on their lives in the same manner. This we pray in the name of Jesus Christ. Amen.

ACTING TO DELIVER

Then the Lord said, "I have seen the affliction of my people who are in Egypt, and have heard their cry because of their taskmasters; I know their sufferings, and I have come down to deliver them out of the hand of the Egyptians, and to bring them up out of that land to a good and broad land, a land flowing with milk and honey."

EXODUS 3:7-8

One of the sweetest sounds to ever fall upon our ears are those of the words, "I love you." It matters not whether they spring from a parent-child relationship or from a man-woman relationship. These words stir the deepest response of which the human heart is capable.

Sad to say, however, after those words are spoken, what may follow often leads to disbelief and dejection. For our actions all too often do not really seem to reflect the love our lips have professed. Disobedient children, abusive parents, exploitive wives, and unfaithful husbands all show that the meaning intended by words of love was only superficial. It is such an experience that sometimes makes us doubt the real meaning intended when words of true love are spoken.

The question arises: How do we translate our reactions to life's events into a response to God's love? If there is one thing clear throughout the Biblical message, it is that God loves us. He loves His people. At the same time, there are legitimate questions raised about the nature of that love based on our human experience.

It was in response to Moses' reaction to God's seeming desertion of Israel that God confronted Moses in his self-imposed exile in Midian. Moses was concerned about his people, who were enslaved in Egypt. It appeared that God just did not care. Then God came with the announcement that He was aware of the affliction Israel was undergoing in Egypt. Thus, one of the first things about God's love we need to recognize is that He does know what kinds of difficulties we are undergoing. He is aware. He does not forget His people. That helps. But, by itself, it is of little value. The suffering still goes on.

Then God announced that He knew the sufferings of His people. In the Old Testament, the verb *to know* always means that which is known by intimate experience. Thus, God was declaring that He had entered into the sufferings of His people. He had not abandoned them, but was suffering with them. That, too, is intensely comforting. We never like to feel abandoned. It helps to have suffering shared.

Yet, even then God's announcement of the nature of His concern did not end. He went on to declare that He was about to deliver the people of Israel from their suffering and to lead them to a better place, the place He had promised them long before. God may not act when we think He should, for His ways are not our ways and what He sees is different from what we see. But God does act to deliver His people. He does not forget His promises. He keeps His Word in redemptive activity. This is the real nature of God's love.

He is aware of suffering, and He enters into our suffering, never abandoning us to it. Furthermore, He also acts to deliver us, keeping His Word to us. In this kind of love we can rest secure.

God of love, we rejoice in gratitude that Thou hast not forsaken us, but hast come through Jesus Christ to deliver us from sin. We pray that Thou wilt help us to trust Thy love and wait for Thy deliverance. Amen.

FOLLOWING THE ONLY DELIVERER

I am the Lord your God from the land of Egypt;
you know no God but me, and besides me there is no savior.

HOSEA 13:4

We Christians love to proclaim the news that God is our Savior. We proudly announce that God has acted in Christ Jesus to redeem us and deliver us. This is just as it should be. God's gracious acts of loving redemption are worth proclaiming. In fact, this is precisely what we have been called to do.

But there is another dimension to that announcement that we must first of all be careful to notice. And, having noticed it, we must be careful to proclaim it as well. This is the fact that God never forces His deliverance on anyone. He offers the way to freedom. God's deliverance of Israel from Egypt would have accomplished nothing if Israel had not followed Him out of Egypt. This is so simple a truth, we often ignore it.

But this is the truth that is reflected in the announcement of the prophet, "You know no God but me." To "know" God is to experience Him, to follow Him, and to obey Him. Thus, the full message of God's redemption of His people includes both the fact that God delivers and the fact that we must follow. Certainly, the theologians are correct when they point out that God makes it possible for us to follow. But He never forces us to follow. He does give us the strength to follow, but He does not drag us kicking and screaming into His redemption.

In addition, there is also a warning to us. There is no one else who can save. Only God saves. Only He offers us a way out of the sin that enslaves and oppresses us. But we must follow wherever He leads. Furthermore, if we do not follow, there is no hope anywhere else.

One of the significant phenomena of our time is the large number of cults springing up all over the country. They are springing up precisely because people do not want to accept God's redemption, but wish to try to find some other means of salvation. It is to people with this attitude that the warning is addressed, "Besides me there is no savior." There is no other way. God alone is the Giver of life. God alone delivers us from the spiritual death into which we have fallen. God alone offers new life. But we must accept it. All the oxygen in the universe is of no use to the person who refuses to breathe.

Likewise, all the life-giving blessings in the universe are of no value to those who refuse to accept them. The gracious good news is that God does deliver us. But the note of warning must always be sounded. The good news, to become life-giving, must be accepted. It is our response to the good news that ultimately determines whether or not it is good news for us.

Merciful God, we thank Thee that Thou dost save us from our sins, giving us new life through Jesus Christ. Yet, Father, we pray that Thou wilt help us not to presume upon Thy love, but to accept it in obedient trust. This we pray in Jesus' holy name. Amen.

More often than not, contemporary Christians speak as if they expected God to do everything for them and for others, with no responsibility laid upon themselves. This idea is foreign to the Biblical message and misunderstands God's love for His people.

Consider, for example, the situation of the Hebrew exiles in Babylon at the time when the Babylonian Empire was overthrown by the Medo-Persians.

> Thus says Cyrus king of Persia, "The Lord, the God of heaven, has given me all the kingdoms of the earth, and he has charged me to build him a house at Jerusalem, which is in Judah. Whoever is among you of all his people, may the Lord his God be with him. Let him go up."
>
> *2 CHRONICLES 36:23*

Now it might be suggested that God could have freed His people from captivity without the intervention of a foreign king. That statement goes without challenge. Of course He could! But that is not the point. Our task is not to discuss or to suggest what God could have done if it had been His will. The point is that God chose to use a human instrument to effect the deliverance of His people. Even more surprising, perhaps, is the fact that God used a foreigner, a pagan king, to finally strike the chains of slavery from off His people. Cyrus became the divine agent of deliverance, even without his own purposes being fully in line with those of God. We know from history that Cyrus allowed all of Babylon's captives to return home if they so desired. He won the friendship of multitudes by granting them freedom and the funds for rebuilding their homeland.

But this is not all there was to the story. When Cyrus issued his edict, giving freedom to the Hebrews, he pointed out that they, too, must bear a part in the rebuilding of the temple in Jerusalem. Once again, human agents were enlisted to carry out the work of God. The temple could certainly have been rebuilt without the efforts of the Hebrew captives in Babylon. But the fact was that they were to have a part.

This brings us face to face with the age-old method of how God accomplishes the work of His kingdom. Surely, an all-powerful God could accomplish anything He wishes without any human aid whatsoever. He can certainly save the world without our help. But the point is, God does not normally act without human instrumentality. He has chosen to allow us the privilege of having a part in His kingdom work. He calls us to be missionaries, to heal the sick, to visit the imprisoned, to be peacemakers, and to offer food and water to the starving and the thirsty. This is apparently not done because God needs us, but because He wants us to share the privilege of laboring with Him.

As a child, I frequently helped my father with many chores around the home. In my childish way, I was sure that he could not have cut the wood or raked the leaves nearly as well without me. But when I became a father, I learned that much help rendered by my children did not ease the task so much as make it more difficult or complex. Yet, I got my children to help me for their good, not for my own. It is this loving motive that apparently moves God to share His kingdom labors with us. We need to have a part in His labors. Therefore, out of His love He gives us this privilege. We become the agents of His ministry of salvation. What a wonderful experience we are allowed to share!

Great God, we thank Thee that Thou hast allowed us to be participants in the great works of Thy kingdom. May we serve even as Jesus did. Amen.

ACTING BECAUSE OF LOVE

Turn, O Lord, save my life;
deliver me for the sake of thy steadfast love.
PSALM 6:4

One of the hardest things you and I have to face in our own self-understanding is that we are really undeserving, unlovely, and unlovable. There is little in us that is really attractive. The reason we have difficulty in accepting this is our personal pride. Somehow, most of us think so highly of ourselves that we cannot understand why we need to be delivered or rescued.

We have grown up with the idea that heaven is a wholly wonderful place where every imaginable good will be present. That being so, we cannot conceive of heaven as being very heavenly if we are not present. Because of this kind of reasoning, we decide that any wise God would certainly include us in His plans of heaven. But this is just not so. In our more honest moments, we must face the fact that we have rebelled against God. We have disobeyed His commands, rejected His will and purpose, and turned consistently to our own way. At the very bedrock of our more serious thought, we must face the fact that there is nothing in us that attracts the interest or wins the favor of God.

Yet, this is precisely what makes the Biblical idea that God loves us so amazing. Even when we are sinners, rebelling against the authority and wisdom of God, He still loves us. And not only does He love us, He has acted from that love to deliver us from the consequences of our sin. Out of that love, He has bridged the gap that we in our sin have created between ourselves and Him. He has come to us in Christ Jesus to save us.

He has saved us from the penalty of sin.

He is saving us from the power of sin.

He will ultimately save us from the very presence of sin.

It is upon this basis of faith and hope that the words of the psalmist rest. He cried out from the agony of his own self-awareness for God's deliverance. But he also knew that his only basis for deliverance rested not in himself but in God's love.

The psalmist was aware of what we too must come to know—God delivers us simply because He loves us, never because we deserve it. If we wait until we deserve God's deliverance, we shall never be delivered. If we wait until we are good enough, or lovable enough, or have God enough in our debt to offer us His salvation, then we shall never ask. The ultimate test of our faith is whether or not we really trust God enough to believe that He loves us. Furthermore, we must believe that His love for us will act in deliverance.

Not only is our only hope in God, but He Himself *is* our hope. I do believe Him when He says that He loves me and that He will deliver me. You and I can trust Him to act for us because He loves us. I might feel more confidence if I felt that God owed me something. But the wonder of His love is that He acts for me when He owes me nothing. Now that is real love.

O loving Father, we thank Thee that Thou hast loved us while we were yet in our sin, and hast acted to deliver us from that which enslaves us. Grant us the full sense of freedom that comes from sin forgiven and from life in fellowship with Thee. This we pray in the name of Him who is Your love in human flesh, even Jesus our Lord. Amen.

---

chapter twelve

The Love That Overwhelms

CHOOSING TO LOVE

Thus says the Lord: "The people who survived
the sword found grace in the wilderness;
when Israel sought for rest, the Lord appeared
to him from afar. I have loved you
with an everlasting love; therefore
I have continued my faithfulness to you.

JEREMIAH 31:2-3

There are times in our lives when we have stumbled into sin and have become so aware of our own guilt and alienation from God that we feel utterly hopeless. Knowing our own unworthiness and sensing our deep need for forgiveness, we are at these times most aware of how difficult it must be for God to love us. Yet, at such times, God comes with His assurance of a love that is ongoing. Regardless of my actions, God's love goes on into the dim unknown.

Israel became aware of the ongoing quality of God's love through their experience with Him in history. Though they time and time again deserved to be utterly cast off, God continued to love them. He would send His judgments upon them, but the intent was to bring Israel back to Himself through repentance. It is this ongoing quality of God's love that probably lies behind the prophetic image of sin as infidelity. Israel's sin was always viewed more as a rejection of God's love than as a violation of His law.

But the Bible always adds another dimension to God's love than its mere endurance. The Biblical writers were fully aware that love without action is nothing more than a superficial emotion. God's love was never viewed that way. Rather, the love of God was always seen as being shown by His loyal acts on their behalf. Though they might reject God, He would not reject them. Though they might turn away from Him, He would not turn away from them.

It is this active quality of God's ongoing love that really gets through to us. He is faithful to His promises, keeping His purposes for us because He loves us. It is this sense of God's faithfulness, springing out of His loving commitment, that serves as the basis for real Christian hope.

It is important to recognize that God's love for us is based on His own commitments of loyalty. The Old Testament writers thoroughly grasped the fact that God's love was a loyal love. They grasped just as firmly that His loyalty was an active loyalty. He had promised to give them His best. He could be trusted to keep His Word. He still can.

The very basis of the Biblical proclamation of God's love is founded on His stedfast loyalty. Human love may not always be dependable. Divine love most certainly is. It is this that makes God's love for us so overwhelming.

In the wonder of Thy love, we turn to Thee, O Lord, accepting Thy love for us with gratitude and amazement. Having experienced Thy love, help us to share both the word of Thy love and the acts of Thy love with others. This we pray in Jesus' name, who showed us Thy love most fully. Amen.

RESPONDING TO OVERWHELMING LOVE

Over and over again, we see evidence that the recurring theme of the Bible is God's abundant love for His people. Yet the theme of His love is no less central than the theme of our expected response to that love.

> Then shall the maidens rejoice in the dance,
> and the young men and the old shall be merry.
> I will turn their mourning into joy,
> I will comfort them, and give them gladness for sorrow.
> I will feast the soul of the priests with abundance,
> and my people shall be satisfied with my goodness,
> says the Lord.
>
> *JEREMIAH 31:13-14*

It is quite intriguing how infrequently we are really satisfied with anything. No matter what comes along, we seem to want more or something bigger and better. It is easy to suggest that such an attitude is simply human nature. Nonetheless, the attitude is present.

We should be struck by God's promise that His people will ultimately be satisfied by His goodness. The thundering note of the prophet's pronouncement is one of exuberant joy. The images of merriment, celebration, and joy simply cannot be escaped.

The basic point behind this is, or so it seems to me, that God's people should find in God's abundant love and grace a real basis for celebration. Can you remember when, as a child, you got an invitation to a birthday party? The anticipation built up until the day finally arrived. Then you went to the party and celebrated with games, songs, and lots of goodies to eat. It was a time of pure celebration.

It is something like this that we should feel when we think of God's love for us. His love bestows us with all sorts of abundant blessings. We are called on to celebrate His abundance, to rejoice at His blessings. Ultimately, we shall find utter satisfaction at the overabundant love of God.

It is from this foundation that one of the key words of contemporary Christianity has become "celebration." God has given us a reason for celebrating.

But this is not the end of the story. We are also called on to share God's abundance and our celebration with others. It is utter selfishness to try to keep good things for ourselves. Instead, we are to share God's blessings, beginning with His love. We are expected to bring others into our celebrations.

It is with this realization that we discover an amazing truth. When we share our joy with another, our joy becomes even greater. Joy shared is joy multiplied. Thus, our satisfaction becomes even deeper, if that is possible.

The Biblical image, then, of our response to divine love is one of utter satisfaction. When we truly experience God, we find our basic needs met. He is wholly satisfying.

Dear God, we thank Thee that Thou hast loved us in Christ Jesus, giving us a reason for celebrating. Help us to find full satisfaction in Thy love through the indwelling presence of Thy Holy Spirit. In Jesus' name we pray and celebrate. Amen.

LOVING THE UNLOVELY

For you are a people holy to the Lord your God; the Lord your God has chosen you to be a people for his own possession, out of all the peoples that are on the face of the earth. It was not because you were more in number than any other people that the Lord set his love upon you and chose you, for you were the fewest of all peoples; but it is because the Lord loves you, and is keeping the oath which he swore to your fathers, that the Lord has brought you out with a mighty hand, and redeemed you from the house of bondage, from the hand of Pharaoh king of Egypt.

DEUTERONOMY 7:6-8

One of the first questions we learn to ask as children is "Why?" As parents, we are at times almost driven to exasperation by our children and by their recurring use of "Why?"

"Why do I have to go to bed?"
"Why is this rose red and that one yellow?"

"Why is the sky blue and the grass green?"
"Why was Mary born before me?"

The list goes on for as long as the child's imagination wonders.

The question "Why?" is perhaps the most useful question in human language. It is in seeking answers to that question that we receive an education. It is in trying to find answers to that question that most of the world's great discoveries have been made.

Therefore, as we become mature, we seek to channel that question into fruitful areas of inquiry. It is not that we quit asking, but it is that we seek to ask in such a way that we can get an answer, or at least begin to find one.

This is as true in spiritual matters as it is in every other area of life. We have noted again and again the Biblical message that God loves us. We have also noted just how astounding that fact is. For in all honesty, there really appears to be little in us for God to love. Thus we ask, "Why?" "Why does God love me?" "Why does God love you?"

Moses, standing before his people on the plains of Moab, anticipated that they were asking just such a question in their hearts. At least, he anticipated that they would like to ask such a question. But the awareness of God's love which originally asks "Why?" very easily slips into an arrogant, spiritual pride as it ponders that love. We assume that God loves us because we deserve that love.

This presumption was fully undercut by Moses' proclamation that God's love for His people had sprung from His own nature, not from anything of value in them. God loves us because He chooses to do so. We cannot earn His love. Neither can we win His love, as if we were trying to woo Him to us. God's love comes to us *because* God is love. It is His own nature to love.

God's love results in good acts toward us. God's love is revealed in His promises, as well as His faithfulness to them. He does not merely promise, He delivers what He has promised. Thus God's love springs forth in mercy. He delivers us from whatever enslaves us, especially our own sinful natures. That is the nature of

God's love. And that is the "why" of God's love. That is what makes His love so amazing. It was true in Moses' day. It is true today. It will be true for all time and eternity. Praise God!

O Thou Lord of love and life, we stand amazed at Thy love for us, and we are eager to share Thy love with others. Send us forth as witnesses; through Jesus Christ, Thy Son, Our Lord, we pray. Amen.

LOVING BEYOND JUDGMENT

How can I give you up, O Ephraim!
How can I hand you over, O Israel!
How can I make you like Admah!
How can I treat you like Zeboim!
My heart recoils within me,
my compassion grows warm and tender.
I will not execute my fierce anger,
I will not again destroy Ephraim;
for I am God and not man,
the Holy One in your midst,
and I will not come to destroy.

HOSEA 11:8-9

It has become common for people not to believe in God sending judgment upon us. The usual thought runs something like this: "If God loves me, then it is inconceivable that He would punish me in such a harsh manner." But this misses the whole point.

First, the very fact that God does send judgment for our sins indicates that He cares. It is indifference that withholds punishment from a disobedient child. The very fact of judgment is an evidence that God cares about you and me.

Furthermore, if we eliminate the passages of judgment from our Bible, we would have to cut out a major portion of the Scriptures. It is worth noting that it is not just the words of the prophets that pronounce judgment. It is also found in the writing of Paul and others of the New Testament authors. Most strikingly, judgment is also found in the teachings of Jesus. The One who most exemplified the love of God clearly speaks of judgment. That God punishes sin is an inescapable fact. It can neither be ignored nor avoided.

But judgment is never the end of the story. The end of the story is God's mercy. God sends judgment out of His justice. But He sends mercy out of His love. Our text portrays for us the cry of a brokenhearted Father. God had judged His people. Punishment had fallen upon them for their sins. But He did not turn them wholly over to judgment. The end was not destruction, but mercy. The mercy of God withheld the fullness of His anger.

We must clearly recognize that God hates sin but He loves sinners. He does not wish to destroy us, but to deliver us. It does not matter that we have difficulty understanding this. So did God's ancient prophet. But the explanation lies in the difference between God and man. You and I might let our anger get out of control, becoming vengeful. But God never allows His wrath to overcome His mercy. His love is still the final word.

Thus it was that Hosea spoke to his people of the God who loved them both through and beyond judgment. And so God is speaking to us today. God's love for His people is still His last word. Judgment is not the end of love; love is the end of judgment.

Gracious God, we cannot comprehend the fulness of Thy love that endures even beyond Thy judgment. Help us to accept the judgments that come as an outpouring of Thy love, bringing us to Thy loving deliverance. Keep us from losing our hope because of sin. Rather, help us to find new hope through Thy compassions. In Jesus' name we pray. Amen.

Surely goodness and mercy shall follow me
all the days of my life; and I shall
dwell in the house of the Lord forever.

PSALM 23:6

Popular Scripture verses are those that speak to the deepest needs of the human heart. It is not without merit, then, that the little psalm from which this verse is taken has been one of the favorites of all time. Even those persons who have never committed their lives to God have found this psalm to offer a sense of sustaining comfort. It surely stands as one of the masterpieces of the world's literature.

Furthermore, this passage itself has become so familiar that its translation in the King James Version of the Bible has affected all subsequent translations. However, as our knowledge of the ancient Hebrew language has grown, we have come to a richer understanding of the meaning of these ancient words.

For example, the word translated "goodness" is far more profound than the English translation might lead us to believe. The word carries with it the idea of God's loyal love, His commitments to His people, and His full purpose to ultimately keep his promises. God does not forget what He has promised to His people. He will accomplish what His ultimate purposes are for us. His loyalty to His commitments can be depended upon both for all time and for eternity.

This goodness, then, springs forth not merely from His love, but from His will. It is His purpose to be loyal. Others may fail, but God never will. Others may turn their backs on us, but God never abandons us. All this is wrapped up in the psalmist's hope in God's goodness.

God's goodness gives us a wonderful hope. But, even more profound, it seems to me, is the thought contained in the expression, "shall follow me." The Hebrew word used here more accurately carries the meaning of "shall pursue me." The hope of the psalmist was not that God's goodness and mercy should follow after him, like an obedient puppy. Rather, the idea is that God's loyal loving kindness and His mercy would actually pursue me, like a hound after its prey. It is not simply that God's love accompanies us throughout our lives, it is rather that God's loyalty and mercy are chasing us. God does not simply bestow these gifts upon us, He actually pursues us to give them to us.

Now that is an overwhelming thought! It excites me to the very innermost part of my being. God is pursuing me to do me good. Even when I rebelliously run from Him, He chases me down. Such is the nature of God's love and loyalty, God does not merely offer me these gifts if I will turn and accept them, He dogs my steps seeking to do His best for me.

Now that is overabundant love! It is the full love that God offers. And it is offered as long as I live. God's love is most vividly understood when we envision Him pursuing us to give Himself to us. That is a real basis for hope and joy. Such should give us utmost confidence in His promises.

Help us, O Lord, that we may not run from Thee in guilt, but may turn to Thee, accepting Thy love, which pursues us down the corridors of time. May we also become Thy servants, pursuing others with Thy love. This we pray in the name of Him who most fully showed us the glory of Thy pursuing love, even Jesus our Lord. Amen.

VOLUNTEERING TO SERVE

And I heard the voice of the Lord saying,
"Whom shall I send, and who will go for us?"
Then I said, "Here am I! Send me."
ISAIAH 6:8

What is it that moves people to volunteer? Obviously, there are countless motives, and they vary depending on the volunteer and the situation.

Therefore, let us focus our question a bit more precisely. What is it that causes people to turn from whatever life's work they have been following in order to serve Christ Jesus as a minister or missionary? What is it that causes people to leave friends, family, and familiar circumstances in order to serve Christ?

The question has many answers. But, in general, couched among the multitudinous answers we might give, there appears to be a common thread, a common idea, which we find in the experience of Isaiah.

Isaiah had apparently approached God with a sense of arrogance, searching for answers to some of his deepest questions about faith and religion. But, when he had actually experienced the awesome holiness of God, his arrogance vanished in an overwhelming sense of guilt. It was at this point that he confessed his sin and experienced God's love in forgiveness and cleansing. In his new relationship with God, he was suddenly aware that God's overwhelming love desired that others should also experience His mercy and forgiveness.

Suddenly, Isaiah was a volunteer. So grateful for God's love was he, that he longed to have the privilege and the opportunity of telling others. It was that simple for him. It should be that simple for us.

The overwhelming love of God for us, which results in our forgiveness and cleansing as well as in a new relationship with God, suddenly becomes a motive for serving Him. Part of the motive is obviously gratitude for what God has done for us. We want some visible, active way by which we can express our thanks. But is is more than mere gratitude, far more. For we are also motivated by the awesome memory of what our situation was before God changed it by His grace. We do not want anyone else to be or to remain in the situation of not really experiencing God's gifts. We wish to become sharers of the message of what God has done for us and what He can and will do for others, as they allow Him.

But even this is not all there is to the story. We are also motivated to volunteer for God's service because we have suddenly experienced something of God's loving concern for all people, and we want to share in that. As we have been forgiven and renewed by God, we discover that our concern for others begins to change. Before, our thoughts were primarily selfish. We turned inward. Now our thoughts are suddenly directed toward the needs of others. Instead of being selfish, we become selfless. Now we turn outward.

Ultimately, however, Isaiah's motive for volunteering was simply that God wanted someone to go for Him. That was enough. If God wanted someone to go in love, he would be that someone.

God does want someone to go now. Will you be that someone?

Help us, O Lord, to respond to Thy call by being a volunteer. This we pray in Jesus' holy name. Amen.

---

chapter thirteen

The Grief That Crushes

LOSING HOPE

> She said to them, "Do not call me Naomi, call me Mara, for the Almighty
> has dealt very bitterly with me. I went away full, and the Lord has
> brought me back empty. Why call me Naomi, when the Lord has af-
> flicted me and the Almighty has brought calamity upon me?"
>
> *RUTH 1:20-21*

These are bitter words springing from a bitter heart. "Do not call
me Naomi [Pleasant], call me Mara [Bitter]." Before we condemn
these words of Naomi, let us consider her plight. She had become
a refugee from her home because of famine, fleeing to Moab, which
was the territory of her enemies. While there, she experienced the
heartbreak of seeing her sons marry foreign girls, of whom she
surely did not approve. But the ultimate tragedies were the death
of her husband and her two sons. She returned home, embittered
by her lot in life and accompanied by a foreign daughter-in-law,
whom she had tried to get to turn back.

"Pleasant" they called her; but "Bitter" she was.

Crushed by grief, she could see nothing but her immediate
sorrow. This, however, is understandable. Grief always crushes.
The greater the grief, the more complete the crushing. And when
grief crushes, we often lash out in bitterness. This is the nature of
grief. But the crushing and the bitterness blind us to the possibil-
ities of what God can do with tragedy. We do God an injustice to

blame Him for our tragedies. But we also do Him an injustice when we forget that He can use our tragedies to accomplish something good.

When the world designs a Calvary, God engineers a resurrection.

Naomi's grief and bitterness caused her to miss the importance of the presence of Ruth. Through Ruth's devotion and love, Naomi ultimately found sustenance, a home, and grandchildren to love and care for. Through Ruth's devotion and love, God provided Israel's greatest king, David (see Ruth 4:13-17). Through Ruth's devotion and love, God provided for the birth of His own Son, Jesus (see Matt. 1:5-6, 16).

Crushing grief is a part of our common existence as humans. We are not excused from it by being Christians. What we are given by being Christians is an awareness that God can and does use our griefs to accomplish His purposes. We can seldom see those purposes at the moment of grief. But we can be rest assured that they are there.

When such grief comes, we, like Naomi, may lose hope for the moment. But we, unlike Naomi, live on this side of the Cross. Thus we can see and know that grief's crushing is never the end of the story. God is at work transforming us from Mara to Naomi, from "Bitter" to "Pleasant." In that we can rest secure. We may be crushed. God isn't. Grief is never the end of the story.

Almighty God, help us who suffer to follow thee through suffering as well as through happiness. Help us to comfort those who do suffer. This we pray in the name of Him who suffered for us, even Jesus, our Lord. Amen.

The Lord said to Samuel, "How long will you grieve over Saul, seeing I have rejected him from being king over Israel? Fill your horn with oil, and go; I will send you to Jesse the Bethlehemite, for I have provided for myself a king among his sons.

1 SAMUEL 16:1

In the world of the circus and the theatre, there is a saying: "The show must go on." By this we mean that, regardless of personal sorrow or tragedy, nothing must be allowed to hinder the presentation of a performance. The clown's heart may be breaking with personal tragedy, but he continues to bring laughter to others. "The show must go on." With such statements we have sought to idolize the performers, to magnify their sacrifice in the face of suffering.

This, in itself, isn't bad. But there is another side to the story. For this concept isn't just confined to the world of entertainment. There is another saying: "Life must go on." It must, you know.

Whatever your personal tragedy, the world does not stop to grieve with you. Friends and family may slow down for a few moments or days. But very quickly, life goes on. And we who grieve must pick ourselves up and go with it, or we get left behind.

Without going into all the background of the relationship between Samuel and Saul, Samuel was clearly overwhelmed with grief by the fact that Saul had been rejected as king. After some length of time, God bluntly said to him, "Get up and get on with the business of life." The world moves on. We must move on with it or be passed by. Furthermore, grief can best be dealt with by action. There is a healing process in doing something. Emotions can be eased by the burning up of physical energy.

There is an old English ballad that tells of a young man who led his troops forth into battle. They loved him dearly and fought valiantly by his side. But in the heat of the fray, he was struck down. Stopping their battle, his loyal followers gathered around their fallen hero.

At this point, he opened his eyes and said,

I'm a little wounded, but I am not slain;
I will lay me down for to bleed a while,
Then I'll rise and fight with you again.
Johnnie Armstrong's Last Goodnight,
John Dryden

So it is when grief crushes us to the ground. We are sorely wounded. But life goes on. So we may lie and bleed awhile, but then we must rise to fight again.

Almighty God, we know that Thou dost understand our griefs and that Thou dost share our sorrows. Help us that we may not allow these griefs to crush us so that we withdraw from life. Rather, let us live to comfort those who sorrow around us. In Jesus' name we pray. Amen.

SORROWING FOREVER

How long, O Lord? Wilt thou forget me forever?
How long wilt thou hide thy face from me?
How long must I bear pain in my soul,
and have sorrow in my heart all the day? . . .

But I have trusted in thy steadfast love;
my heart shall rejoice in thy salvation.
I will sing to the Lord,
because he has dealt bountifully with me.
PSALM 13:1-2a, 5-6

There come into our lives those griefs that seem to be without end. We wish to join in with the psalmist and cry out, "How long?" Sitting for days, weeks, and months beside the bed of a dying loved one, we wish to cry out, "How long?" The visitation of death, at least, is final; it focuses grief into a point. But most sorrows are much more extended. A rebellious child, an unfaithful husband, or any life situation that brings daily experience of grief becomes utterly overwhelming. What can we do with it, then?

We can rebel, striking out feebly and futilely against whatever or whoever brings our grief. Yet this seldom brings relief. Rather, the obvious futility of such actions seems only to plunge us deeper into the grief.

We can piously acquiesce, mouthing the right words of spiritual devotion, while the rage and anger within our hearts well up to burst forth in a flood of hatred and hostility. But what does this accomplish?

We can also wring our hands in helplessness, bewailing the lot that time and circumstance have thrust upon us. Yet no one listens.

All these can be our response to ongoing grief. We may have tried them all or have known someone who has. None of them was effective in dealing with grief.

However, the psalmist did find a solution, and he shares it with us. He neither denied his grief nor rebelled against it. He carried his need to God. In so doing, the grief became no less real and certainly no less overwhelming. But he did discover (or remind himself) that there was a past relationship with God that could sustain him. His life had been built upon trusting God. That same trust could sustain him in his present condition. He had rejoiced with God in the past; he would again rejoice in the future. There had been times of song in the past; there would be times of song in the future.

The faith that sustains us in the time of overwhelming grief is the faith that remembers the past with God and therefore has hope for the future. In the midst of such grief, sorrow appears to be endless. But, and this is important, in the midst of such grief, we are not alone!

Being a Christian does not excuse us from the common griefs of humanity. But being a Christian does give us the companionship of One who will not leave us alone in our suffering. Such grief, then, may overwhelm us, but it will not destroy us.

It is not deliverance from grief but strength in grief that we are promised. That is enough.

O God, Thou who hast suffered for us, help us also to know that Thou dost suffer with us. May we know the comfort of Thy presence as we walk through the valleys of life. This we pray in the name of Jesus Christ, Thy Son, our Lord. Amen.

CRYING TO EXHAUSTION

Save me, O God! For the waters
have come up to my neck.
I sink in deep mire, where there is no foothold;
I have come into deep waters,
and the flood sweeps over me.
I am weary with my crying; my throat is parched.
My eyes grow dim with waiting for my God.

PSALM 69:1-3

Grief can crush us in a number of ways. It can crush us by a sudden swift onslaught. It can also crush us when it appears to drag on and on, with no prospect of any relief. But it also crushes when it plunges us to such depths of despair that we weep ourselves into utter exhaustion. At such times, we weep until there is no strength left. We are overwhelmed, swamped, about to go under for the last time, and we are just too weary to produce another tear, to lift our voice again.

What then? Shall we just lie back and sink?

No! Not at all! When I have wept myself to exhaustion, God is not exhausted. When I am too weak to cry out again, there is

One who still knows my condition. I am not alone, even when I feel alone.

Thus the psalmist can also say, "But I am afflicted and in pain; let thy salvation, O God, set me on high! . . . For the Lord hears the needy, and does not despise his own that are in bonds." (Ps. 69:30-33). With these words, the psalmist set forth his assurance that the God who is with us in good times can also sustain us in bad times. My weakness is no indication of God's weakness. Even when I am exhausted by grief, God isn't. Though I cannot lift myself up from whatever situation has overcome me, God can "set me on high."

We must note that what sustained the psalmist was not God's deliverance, but the assurance that He could deliver. We can face whatever comes as long as we know that we are not alone, that we have not been forsaken. God can deliver. If He doesn't, then I can endure whatever comes with the assurance of His awareness, His presence, and His suffering with me.

God does not always answer our prayers uttered from the pit of overwhelming grief. But His silence is not evidence that He cannot answer or that He does not care. When His own Son hung on the Cross, crying out, "My God, my God, why hast thou forsaken me?" (Matt. 27:46), God did not openly respond. But it wasn't that He couldn't. Rather, He entered into Jesus' suffering, accompanying Him, and using His anguish. So He does with us.

When I am utterly exhausted by my grief, I am still assured that God is with me, and that He can make something out of my grief. I am not alone. It is this that sustains me. It can sustain you too.

Father, help us to know that Thy silence is not an indication that Thou dost not care. As we discover this, we may bear witness to it before others. In Christ's name we pray. Amen.

BEARING OUR GRIEFS

Surely he has borne our griefs and
carried our sorrows;
yet we esteem him stricken, smitten
by God, and afflicted.

ISAIAH 53:4

Grief is more easily borne when it is shared. We all have experienced this at one time or another. A message of death comes to you when you are far from home. It is far more overwhelming while you are separated from your loved ones. As the family gathers, the grief becomes no less real. But it does become easier to bear because you are sharing it with those you love and who love you. This makes our text more meaningful.

The prophet has drawn a magnificent portrait of God's Suffering Servant. While we treasure its images, sometimes we miss some of its more profound truths. One of these oft-neglected truths is that God's Servant bears our griefs.

The prophet, centuries before the ministry of Jesus, was looking forward in hope. We, living centuries on this side of that same ministry, can see how God fulfilled His ancient promises. But, even though we can see the fulfillment, let us beware of missing a major fact.

Among all else that Jesus accomplished, not the least was that He entered into life as it really is. He played the game by the same rules we do. In so doing, He learned about human sorrow.

Almost certainly, He has experienced the death of Joseph, entering into that experience of grief. He had wept outside the tomb of His friend Lazarus, sharing the grief of Mary and Martha. He had also entered into the grief of Jairus and his wife when their daughter had died. And He also interrupted the funeral procession of the only son of the widow of Nain. He experienced grief at the hardheartedness of His disciples and also knew the grief of betrayal. Furthermore, He knew the grief at being forsaken by His friends on the night of His arrest. Grief was His companion, even as it is ours.

But He not only knew grief in the past, He shares our griefs now! We are not alone. He enters into our suffering, sustaining us with His presence, undergirding us through the process of shared grief. Whenever grief comes, He shares it in love.

By sharing our griefs, He makes them easier to bear. The burden becomes somewhat less heavy. He accompanies us as we walk in the valley of the shadow of deep darkness. It is this assurance that sustains us when grief crushes.

The prophet offered his people the assurance of Immanuel, which means "God with us" (see Isa. 7:14). This assurance is ours. He is with us. He bears our griefs. This is our faith. It is enough.

O God of grace and mercy, help us to know that we are never alone in our sorrows, that Thou art with us. And when we have passed through that valley together, may we share the truth of "God with us" in witness to others. Through Jesus Christ we pray. Amen.

SUFFERING FOR SIN

Yet it was the will of the Lord to bruise him;
he has put him to grief; when he makes himself
an offering for sin, he shall see his offspring,
he shall prolong his days;
the will of the Lord shall prosper in his hand;
he shall see the fruit of the travail
of his soul and be satisfied; by his knowledge
shall the righteous one, my servant,
make many to be accounted righteous;
and he shall bear their iniquities.

ISAIAH 53:10-11

Grief turns our thoughts inward. That is understandable, for grief makes us hurt. And when we hurt, our whole being focuses itself on the pain. But at a time when we are not personally crushed by grief, we need to ponder the image our text sets before us.

Again, we know the ultimate fulfillment of this portrait. It is Jesus. But the prophet did not know the story of Jesus. By the inspiration of God, he was given one of the greatest revelations man ever received. It was that God's Servant was going to take upon Himself the sins of others, suffering for those sins. Here is the perfect portrait of vicarious suffering: the innocent suffering for the guilty.

How often have we stood beside the bed of a suffering loved one, wishing that we could take the pain into ourself. This is a common experience of human love.

I have watched my children suffer and wished I could bear their pain. I have watched my wife suffer and wished I could bear her pain. I have watched my mother suffer and longed to be able to bear her pain. But I could not.

Yet God's Servant saw us suffering under the burdens of our sin and took them upon Himself. He not merely suffered for us, He who was innocent took upon Himself our guilt. This is a striking picture. It moves us deeply. Voluntarily, He took upon Himself the pain of our sins. Now *that* is love! It is love indeed!

Perhaps of all the people who lived when Jesus did, there was only one who really realized on the morning of the crucifixion what was really happening. That was Barabbas. He had been condemned to die, but was spared. He alone could look at Jesus on the Cross and know that Someone was suffering for him, dying in his place. Barabbas alone knew that the Cross of Jesus had been intended for him.

From this side of the Cross, our knowledge and experience are not so limited. We all know that Jesus died for us. He suffered for you and me, bearing our sins. May we, in turn, learn to live for Him. Since He suffered for us, we should live our lives for Him.

Help us, O Lord, to pause in wonder at Thy love for us, which drove Jesus to suffer for us and with us. Now may we so love Him in return, that we live our lives for Him, suffering for and with others. In Jesus' name we pray. Amen.

chapter fourteen

The Hope That Sustains

LOOKING BEYOND THE PRESENT

And the surviving remnant of the house of Judah shall again take root downward, and bear fruit upward; for out of Jerusalem shall go forth a remnant, and out of Mount Zion a band of survivors. The zeal of the Lord will do this.

2 KINGS 19:30-31

In the darkest periods of life, God calls us to lift our eyes beyond the present and view the future He has planned. At a time when the people of Judah felt that all hope was gone, when it looked as if the armies of Assyria were surely about to overwhelm them, they were urged to look beyond the immediate catastrophe. All was not lost! God was still in control. They were assured that there would be a "surviving remnant."

Sometimes, when the days appear to be blackest, mere survival is an accomplishment. But there was more hope for Israel than this, much more. Life was going to be fruitful again. God's promises included renewed roots and renewed fruit. Often, evangelists preaching a superficial Gospel have offered the world peace, success, and prosperity if people would simply turn to God. Such is hardly a Biblical picture. Being a Christian never excuses us from the crises of life. War, disease, tragedy, heartache, sickness, and death—all these come to the Christian just as they do to the non-Christian. The difference, and the only difference, that is really offered is that, for the Christian, life will never become rootless or fruitless. God's presence does sustain us through the crises that come.

This is the main point. History never destroys God. It may dim our vision of God. It may even destroy our false images of God. But the God of the Bible is the Victor over history, not its Victim. And even when, as at Calvary, God seems to become the ultimate Victim, there is the resurrection beyond, when we see Him as Victor.

It was this hope for the future that caused the prophet to see God's people not coming to Zion but going out from the city of God. Not only would they survive with roots and fruit, they would be messengers that God is able to sustain through the crises of life. It is not for ourselves alone that God sustains, it is also that we may share this news with others. The view beyond the present is one of God's people bearing witness to His sustenance.

The hope that causes us to see beyond the present is not a fanciful dream, but a realistic vision. For it is not based on some dream of pie in the sky by and by when you die, it is based upon the assurance that God's zeal, His passionate love for His creatures, will fulfill His plans and purposes. God's people shall be sustained through tragedy because He loves them. God's people shall bear witness of that sustaining vision of the future because He loves others. Undergirding the vision is God's love for all mankind. That is sufficient.

O Thou God of love, shine the light of Thy love into the darkness of our present crises, that we may see the view of Thy tomorrow beyond the darkness of today. Amen.

PROMISING A NEW RELATIONSHIP

Behold, the days are coming, says the Lord, when I will make a new covenant with the house of Israel and the house of Judah. . . . I will

> put my law within them, and I will write it upon their hearts; and I will
> be their God, and they shall be my people. And no longer shall each
> man teach his neighbor and each his brother, saying, "Know the Lord,"
> for they shall all know me, ... for I will forgive their iniquity, and I
> will remember their sin no more.
>
> *JEREMIAH 31:31-34*

Sooner or later, there comes to every one of us the awareness of lost innocence, the realization of sin and rebellion, the overwhelming burden of guilt. We become fully aware that by our own actions we have severed our relationship with God. We then seek to cover up our own failures by bluster, by hostility toward God and all things godlike, and by vain attempts to lose ourselves in activity, achievement, and acclaim.

But God in His wondrous love for us, even in the midst of our sin, comes offering a new relationship. To ancient Israel and to modern humankind alike, God offers a new covenant. This is probably the most theologically profound concept in the entire Old Testament. Jesus Himself chose this image of a new relationship to define for His disciples what He was doing in His own life and death. The term itself has become the actual title of the second half of our bible—the New Testament, which is simply a different way of translating "new covenant."

The new relationship is initiated by God and is based on His forgiveness of our sin. At the point of God's forgiveness, the new covenant concept first makes contact with our predicament. We need to be forgiven. Yet the most shocking aspect of God's forgiveness is that *He forgets our sin.* The father who welcomes the prodigal son does not throw up to him past rebellions. The past is forgiven and forgotten!

This new relationship is also an inner one. It begins within the human consciousness. It is not a matter of external laws of behavior; it is a matter of personal experience. As we have previously stated, in the Old Testament, the verb *to know* always refers to that which is learned by personal experience, not what is learned merely by rote. This new relationship, thus, is established

147

through our own personal experience with God. God is no longer One about Whom we merely learn, He is One whom we meet! This does not mean that I cannot learn much about God. What it does mean is that my personal relationship with Him is established through meeting Him.

But this relationship does have its laws. Through our personal experience with God, His will becomes imbedded within our conscience. We do not relate to Him through obedience, but we do demonstrate our relationship to Him through obedience. It is this new relationship that offers hope to sustain us when we are overwhelmed by guilt. Because of this, we can truly say, "All my sins are gone!" God has come with newness.

Almighty God, Thou who spoke to other peoples in ancient days, speak to us in these days with hope of newness. Help us to know and to share that we are not captives of the past, but have been freed for the future. In Jesus' name we pray. Amen.

USING THE OPPORTUNITY

And who knows whether you have not come
to the kingdom for such a time as this?
ESTHER 4:14b

The threat of catastrophe or crisis is frequently more frightening than the real thing. The fear of the imagined danger is often more terrifying than facing the actual enemy. While this is true, when real dangers and difficulties do come, we seldom feel prepared to face them adequately. What are we to do at such times?

In the setting of our text, an edict had been issued ordering the total annihilation of all the Jews in Persia. Queen Esther, a Jewess, was afraid to approach her husband, the king, for no one could enter his presence uninvited without facing the threat of immediate death. It was as she faced this dilemma that her foster father suggested that the time might be one of opportunity for her rather than threat.

The rest of the story is really immaterial at this juncture. We know that she emerged from this crisis victorious, but that is beside the point for our discussion here. For Esther, the entire situation was altered by the way in which she viewed it. She was called on to view her crisis as an opportunity rather than as a catastrophe. And so it is with us.

Over and over again, the Scriptures bear witness to similar situations. For Jesus in Gethsemane, He could have faced the Cross as the catastrophic ending of His life and ministry or as the opportunity of serving God in fulfilling His redemptive plan. He chose to see it as the will of God, as an opportunity. For Paul, the numerous crises of his life could have been wept over as catastrophic to his ministry or as opportunities for service. Over and over again, we see him accepting them as opportunities.

The events will not change. The situation will stay the same. The only thing that can alter them, then, is how we view them. Are such experiences catastrophes or opportunities? Are they defeats or doorways to victory?

For Esther, the whole purpose of her life was to be found in seeing a catastrophe as an opportunity. But it was not enough merely to see the possibility of an opportunity. She had to use the opportunity to serve God.

Looking back to our yesterdays, we can recognize all sorts of opportunities that were presented to us but which we failed to use. We may even have seen them as opportunities, but failed to respond properly, not seizing and using them. The priest and the Levite in Jesus' parable of the Good Samaritan both saw the opportunity to help the wounded man. Yet neither one did anything. It is our responsibility and opportunity to find a sustaining hope in the midst of crisis, by looking for the opportunities they provide. That there are such opportunities in every crisis should give us hope.

O God who created this world, help us live in it as we are, both seeing and using the opportunities that the common crises of humanity afford us for Thy loving service. This we pray for Christ's sake. Amen.

PARDONING GUILT

For thy name's sake, O Lord,
Pardon my guilt, for it is great.

PSALM 25:11

It goes without special notice that we do not ask anyone to do anything we do not believe that he or she is able to do. I do not go to a hardware store for medicine, nor do I go to a restaurant for lumber. The same thing is true when we apply it to the realm of the spiritual.

The Biblical hymn from which our text comes reflects the fact that the psalmist was overwhelmed by his own sense of guilt. In that, we can identify with him. Having done wrong, he knew it. He was quite aware of the sense of guilt and alienation that had come as a result. Sin had served to separate him from God. And so it does with us.

Furthermore, his sense of sin only served to point out the holy nature of God in contrast to his own. You and I also experience the same thing.

My faithlessness causes me to become more aware of God's faithfulness.

My indifference and coldness cause me to become more aware of God's loving concern.

My unbending hardness causes me to become more aware of God's mercy.

And so it goes. The sense of sin and guilt alienates me even further from God. The sense of God's goodness and mercy plunges me even further into despair as I ponder my own rebellious stubbornness.

But—and the psalmist knows this quite well—this same awareness of the nature of God's love, mercy, and stedfastness also serves as the basis for hope. For hope is not based on me, but on God. Hope based on my own abilities is little more than a fleeting vision, a dream that disappears when I face the realities of life. But hope based on God is an anchor that holds me through all the storms of life.

So it is, then, that I can cry out to God from the midst of my guilt,

> For thy name's sake, O Lord,
> Pardon my guilt, for it is great.

This is a hope that sustains me in my sinful weakness. It does not fully scatter all the darkness of my sin. But it does shine into the darkness of my despair.

Because of my sin, I am guilty. But God be praised, because of God's love, I can be pardoned. That is hope. It is hope, indeed!

O Thou who didst shine the light of Thine order into the darkness of chaos, bringing the worlds into being, now shine the light of Thy love into the darkness of my guilt, bringing my hope to fruition. May I never be content to walk in darkness, but help me to seek the light of Thy loving face. For this I pray in Jesus' name. Amen.

TRUSTING THROUGH TROUBLE

God is our refuge and strength,
a very present help in trouble. . . .
The Lord of hosts is with us;

the God of Jacob is our refuge. . . .
The Lord of hosts is with us;
the God of Jacob is our refuge.

PSALM 46:1, 7, 11

It is of no more use trying to find an actual historical occasion for a psalm from its content than it is to identify such an occasion for a hymn in a contemporary hymnal merely by reading its words. Hymns have survived because they speak to the common needs of human experience. The same is true of the psalms. Many occasions have been suggested for the words of our text. They may all be probable, but these words have lived because they speak for everyone. They especially speak for you and me.

Life as it is has many troubles. The catalog of natural catastrophes, of human tragedies, of sorrows, heartaches, and griefs is quite large. We have all been there. No one of us has escaped our share of sorrow. But the persons who belong to God have found that when these troubles come, they do not have to be faced alone. In this, the psalmist found strength and offers it to us. He found a resting place in God. He offers that resting place to us, in confident hope.

But there is a striking addition to the psalmist's basis for hope. Normally, we would expect the Old Testament to say: "The God of Abraham, Isaac, and Jacob is our refuge. Or perhaps we might find: "The God of our fathers is our refuge." But this psalm twice uses the surprising phrase: "The God of Jacob is our refuge." We must question why such an expression is used instead of one of the more expected phrases.

The answer may rest in our understanding of the kind of person Jacob was. He was a supplanter, a trickster from the beginning. He was the confidence man *par excellence*, always out to turn a fast buck, always out to get something for nothing. In his early and middle years, there was little in the life of Jacob that was exemplary or admirable. But somehow, along the way, God got hold of Jacob and transformed him into a prince of God. That was a miracle of grace, mercy, and forgiveness. It is precisely Jacob's experience that offered hope to the psalmist. It also offers hope to us. *The God who can use a man like Jacob can use me too!* Now that is a real basis for hope. The God who transformed Jacob can transform me too! In that simple little fact I can find strength to face any crisis. Truly, "the God of Jacob is our refuge." That is worth repeating. It is also worth believing.

Gracious God, help us who find life's defeats so threatening to find sustaining strength and hope in the knowledge that Thou art our refuge in every trouble. For Jesus' sake we pray. Amen.

DELIVERING THE NEEDY

For he delivers the needy when he calls,
the poor and him who has no helper.
He has pity on the weak and the needy,
and saves the lives of the needy.
From oppression and violence he redeems their life;
and precious is their blood in his sight.

PSALM 72:12-14

When most contemporary Americans hear the word *needy*, we immediately think of someone who is impoverished, probably someone who is on welfare and really deserves to be. We almost always think of a person who is seriously lacking in money and the things it will buy. There is nothing wrong with this image, except that it is far too limited. To the psalmist, the "needy" did include those who were penniless. But the "needy" also included those who were alone, those who had no other human person to whom to turn. Furthermore, the "needy" also included the weak. This probably included both those who were physically infirm as well as those who were spiritually helpless. Even beyond this, the "needy" were those whose lives were in danger; and the danger could come either from physical enemies, natural catastrophes, or some dread disease.

The "needy," therefore, appear quite clearly to have been those with any kind of need that they could not meet in and of themselves. That, at times, certainly includes you and me. But it also includes, at one time or another, everyone else as well. We are all needy. Yet we seldom see our common brotherhood in this. When we do not feel our own need, we far too frequently fail to sense our brother's need. When we are weak, we are so wrapped up in our own need that we do not grasp the needs of others. How tragic!

But God is not like this. He both sees and knows our need. Furthermore, because of His love, He enters into our need to do something about it. To the Old Testament psalmist, the verb *to redeem* meant to act as the next of kin. Thus, when he said that God "redeems their life," he was saying that God makes Himself our next of kin. He voluntarily adopts us Himself, becoming our closest relation.

Furthermore, because God relates Himself to us, we become aware that we are precious in His sight. Now that is a real basis for hope! God sees value in us. I am precious to Him! You are precious to Him!

Whatever my need, however difficult my situation has become, I am important to God. In fact, I am so important that He begins to meet my need by adopting me into His family. The God who created this universe by His word of power, bends down and adopts the needy, becoming our next of kin. That is a basis for a hope that can sustain you and me in any time of need.

Almighty God, we cannot comprehend Thy love which bends down to us in our need. But we do rejoice in that love, finding it sufficient for all our need. Help us to bear witness to that love, seeking to bring it to bear in reaching others who are needy before Thee. We pray this in the name of Him who became our elder Brother, even Jesus our Lord. Amen.

---

chapter fifteen

The Mercy That Conquers

HEALING THE INCURABLE

> For thus says the Lord: Your hurt
> is incurable, and your wound is grievous. . . .
> For I will restore health to you, and your wounds
> I will heal, says the Lord,
> because they have called you an outcast:
> "It is Zion, for whom no one cares!"
>
> *JEREMIAH 30:12, 17*

There are few things that strike more terror to the human heart than the words: "I am sorry, but your disease is incurable." When the doctor announces that, all your hopes and dreams come crashing into the dust. It does not matter that you have known all along that life had its limits. As long as the limit remained safely undefined, you could keep your own finitude safely packed away in the inner recesses of your mind. But with the doctor's announcement, it has suddenly been brought up from its hiding place and emblazoned on your immediate horizon.

It is no less frightening to the sensitive spirit to be told that our spiritual life is just as limited. Yet, the constant message of the prophets to Israel was that their sin condition was incurable. The same is true of us. You and I may think (and we usually do) that we can turn from our sin and our sins at any time. We may think (and we usually do) that we can somehow do enough good things and accomplish enough personal reforms to make ourselves both attractive and necessary to God.

It is, then, quite a shock to be brought up short with the announcement that our spiritual condition is incurable. Not all the good works in the world can make us spiritually clean. Not all of our lofty thoughts or good intentions can accomplish this either. But more importantly, neither can all of the religion in the world. We ourselves can do nothing about our spiritual disease. It is wholly incurable from any human standpoint.

It is this pronouncement that plunges us into spiritual despair, or else it causes us to give up striving for improvement and to lose ourselves in thoughtless and careless living. It is at this point that God comes on the scene with His announcement that He can and will heal the spiritually incurable. What we cannot do for ourselves, He will do for us. He *can* do it because He is God. He *will* do it because He cares for us. This is the way of the divine mercy. God loves His people. He despises sin but never the sinner.

The basis, then, for any spiritual hope is neither our good works nor our multiplied religious activity. Spiritual hope that offers life beyond our rebelliousness is based only on God's loving mercy.

The world looks at the outcast and downtrodden and says, "No one cares!" But the world is wrong. God looks at the same outcast and downtrodden and tenderly says, "I care!" And He does. Therefore He will and does cure our incurable sinfulness out of His abundant, all-conquering mercy. That is hope.

Merciful God, help us to turn both from our sin and from our striving to overcome our sin to Thee, that we may find forgiveness for our rebellion and strength to be faithful to Thee. This we pray in the name of Jesus, our Lord. Amen.

> Behold, I will gather them from all the countries to which I drove them in my anger and my wrath and in great indignation; I will bring them back to this place, and I will make them dwell in safety. And they shall be my people, and I will be their God.
>
> *JEREMIAH 32:37-38*

The wrath of God toward sin and the judgment of God upon sinners are major themes of both the Old and New Testaments. Sometimes it is suggested that such descriptive passages are foreign to the Spirit of Christ and denigrating to the concept of God. But before we pass such a judgment, we need to read again the messages of the Old Testament prophets. They are all filled with such pronouncements. Even those passages of love and comfort, such as in Hosea and in Isaiah 40-66, are filled with the announcement of doom and destruction.

The New Testament, contrary to many common ideas, is no less filled with words of judgment. Even Jesus Himself, regularly described in terms of gentle meekness, had His moments of heated indignation and intense wrath. And His words of judgment are scathing denunciations.

When we consider the warnings of wrath and judgment in the Bible, we usually fail to realize that these are seldom described in terms of being God's *final* Word to His people. The Old Testament clearly sees God's hand at work in the temporal judgments that came to Israel. But what is seen, along with punishment, is primarily redemption. The Old Testament prophets saw God sending judgment to awaken Israel to the danger of the paths the people were following. Thus, the intention was to cause them to turn back to God. Yet even this was not their last word about judgment.

Not only was God seeking to lead Israel to repentance, He also promised to come after them. The worst judgments described in the Old Testament were usually in the form of exile, captivity, and slavery. To those people, once they had been carried away from the land, they had been carried away from God. The prophets had to show them that God was the sovereign Lord of all the earth, and that He reached out to them wherever they were. The ultimate end of this message of God's sovereignty was that God would seek them out wherever they were, and that He would deliver them from their captivity. Furthermore, not only would God deliver them, He would also protect them, making them to "dwell in safety."

Now that message was wonderful enough to a people in exile. But the best part of God's promised mercy was that there would be a new relationship established between Him and His people.

To us who know that the greatest captivity and enslavement is not physical but spiritual, these promises of God offer no less hope. He promises to deliver from slavery to sin and from the judgment of sin all those who will follow Him. This is done by the new relationship that He establishes with us. It is imperative to note that it is not we who establish a new relationship with God, but God who establishes it with us. We do not make God our God. He makes us His people. We do not make ourselves His loyal followers. He makes Himself our sovereign Lord. What is impossible for us is possible with God. This is the message of His conquering mercy.

Gather us, O Lord, from the sin that enslaves us, bringing us to Thyself through Thy love. We wait in hope for Thy deliverance. This we pray through Jesus Christ, Thy Son, our Lord. Amen.

LOVING FREELY

I will heal their faithlessness;
I will love them freely,
for my anger has turned from them.

HOSEA 14:4

Ask a small child how much she loves you, and she might extend her arms to their farthest reach and say, "I love you this much!" As we grow older, we discover that love cannot be measured spatially. Then we begin to measure love in other ways. Sometimes we measure love by the cost of the gifts our loved one brings or that we give. Or perhaps we measure love by the amount of sacrifice our loved one makes for us. Almost without variation, we more "mature" adults measure love by its cost or by its price.

Now we really know that love cannot be measured in such a way. Yet, we still try to apply some sort of "price" measurement to love. It is against this kind of background that we need to understand God's declaration of love through His prophet Hosea.

Anything that can be measured is limited. The very measurement is its limit. God communicates to us that His love for His people cannot be so measured. It is without limits. The amazing truth of God's mercy is that it is unlimited. There are no spatial limits to God's love. Nor are there any value limits to god's love. There are just no limits of any kind to God's love. Thus there is the clear assurance of the bountifulness of God's love. We can rest secure in the realization that God's love is always overabundant. It is beyond our comprehension.

Not only is God's love unlimited, it is also without price. It is easy to say that the price God paid for our redemption was the death of His Son. That is certainly true. But let us never speak of it as if that were all it cost Him. God's love for us costs Him throughout all eternity. Its value is immeasurable because its cost is immeasurable.

But the adverb in Hosea's proclamation cannot even be dismissed with this kind of treatment. Since the love of God is so great as to be without cost, it is offered to us without price! There is no price by which we can repay God's love, or by which we can buy it. Thus, God offers it equally to everyone. We are not denied His love because of our inability to earn it. He does not love us because we have won His love, but because He loves us from His own nature.

In addition, we need also to recognize that this unlimited love that is freely bestowed on us is an active love. It draws us back to God in faithfulness, for He heals our faithlessness. He makes it possible for us to be faithful to Him. Ponder that thought for a moment. God not only brings us into a new and right relationship with Himself, He makes it possible for us to maintain that relationship. He cleanses us of sin and guilt, removes our faithlessness, and gives us the spiritual health to be faithful.

Now that is real love. God's love is not cheap love. Its value is so great that it is beyond measurement. Having received it, we can only offer our own love in return.

O Thou who hast loved us throughout all time and hast shown us that love incarnate in Jesus Christ, help us to love Thee also beyond measure, and to show that love by loving Thy people in the same manner. Help us to make our love active by doing good for others. This we pray in the holy, loving name of Jesus, Thy Son, our Lord. Amen.

REDEEMING BEYOND JUDGMENT

> Who is a God like thee, pardoning iniquity
> and passing over transgression for the remnant
> of his inheritance? He does not retain his anger
> for ever because he delights in steadfast love.
> He will again have compassion upon us,
> he will tread our iniquities under foot.
> Thou wilt cast all our sins into the depths of the sea.
> *MICAH 7:18-19*

Ancient Israel lived in a world that was believed to be inhabited by a multiplicity of gods. Every nation that existed alongside of her had numerous gods. To Israel's people, Micah announced that there was not one of the many gods who could be compared with the God of Israel. He was unique. Later, they came to realize that He was the only God.

Our Western culture faces a wholly different world. Our world does not generally believe in many gods. Instead, atheism and agnosticism are more the rule of the day. In general, people in our secular society do not believe in any god; or, if they do, they do not believe that we can know anything about the god. To our society, Micah announces that God does exist and that He can be known.

Micah's major message was one of judgment upon the sinful injustices of His people. They acted as if God did not exist. So Micah pronounced a coming doom upon those who were unfaithful to God by being unjust to their neighbors.

At the same time, Micah did not leave either his people or us hanging on the false idea that judgment was God's final word to His people. To the prophet, God's temporal judgment was always limited.

Beyond the judgments of time, the prophet saw pardon, stedfast love, and compassion. This can be seen in God's cleansing of our sin. It is both pardoned and removed. That is both the beginning and the end of God's love for us. Sin is gone. This is not because we become good but because God is merciful.

The high point of the prophetic hope, however, rested in the stedfast love and compassion of God. It is because of this that He cleanses us. It is God's intent that we should live in the experience of both His love and mercy. These were never merely ideas about God which we should hold on to. Rather, the prophet always saw these as the actual way God lived with us. This is still true. Whatever we experience of God, it is always a part of His love and mercy. Furthermore, we experience these beyond immediate crises because He redeems us beyond His judgment. Judgment is real. There is no doubt of that. But the last word is always that of merciful cleansing.

God comes into our lives to make things right. This does not mean that we shall have abundant wealth, lives of ease, and an existence free from pain and suffering. What it does mean is that we shall discover that the guilt that separated us from God is gone. It is that simple. With guilt gone, we can be aware of God's loving presence within our lives. Then we can walk into whatever the future brings hand in hand with God. We have been restored by His love. That is all-conquering mercy.

Merciful God, we praise Thee for the mercy that delivers us from the judgment on our sins, cleansing us and taking us into Thy presence. We lift our prayer to Thee through Jesus Christ. Amen.

TURNING JUDGMENT INTO MERCY

Then the Lord God said, "Behold, the man has become like one of us, knowing good and evil; and now, lest he put forth his hand and take also of the tree of life, and eat, and live forever"—therefore the Lord God sent him forth from the garden of Eden, to till the ground from which he was taken. He drove out the man; and at the east of the garden of Eden he placed the cherubim, and a flaming sword which turned every way, to guard the way to the tree of life.

GENESIS 3:22-24

From time immemorial, humankind has paused before this story to agonize over the loss experienced through our primal ancestors. The flaming sword wielded by the cherubim, guardians of God's holiness, has been seen as an image of judgment upon all of us, barricading the way to eternal life. We have viewed this scene as descriptive of God's judgment on our sinful rebellion. We have understood it as clearly saying that the consequence of our sin has been the loss of access to God and to life.

Now that is true. These are precisely the consequences of our sin. But there are other things that we must note at this point. We should first of all remember that the story tells how the man and his wife hid from God after their sin. It is not God who drives us from Himself when we sin. Rather, it is we who immediately separate ourselves from Him. So the image of the flaming sword is not simply a symbol of our alienation from God. That has already been noted earlier in the accounts. Then what is its significance?

The image of the sword is not simply a symbol of judgment, although it certainly includes that meaning. We do lose access to God and to spiritual life as a consequence of our sin. But there is a more significant meaning to the sword.

Some non-Christians boldly say, "You Christians offer me eternal life. Well, I don't want it. I might enjoy living for an extra few years, but I cannot think of anything more horrible than living forever just as my life is now."

Such an attitude helps to clarify the point I wish to make. The spiritual life the Bible offers is not simply more of the same kind of existence we now have; it is a life that is *worth* living. The flaming sword symbolizes that God does not want His people to live forever in an alienated condition. He therefore barricaded the way to the tree of life, to eternal life, until He could first deliver His people from their guilt. Viewed in this way, we suddenly see the flaming sword as an image of God's mercy, not merely of His judgment.

This is the real evidence of the loving mercy of God. He even transforms judgment into mercy. The symbols of wrath also become symbols of love. That is the depth and breadth and height of God's love. He does not and will not leave us in our sinful, alienated condition. Rather, He protects us from ourselves until we have a chance to respond to the ultimate message of His love. God's judgment is real. But so is His mercy. And His mercy ultimately conquers.

Gracious God, forgive us for our sin, granting to us both cleansing and restoration. May we come to know the quality of life that is worth going on, through Jesus Christ; for it is in His name that we pray. Amen.

DEFEATING ALL ENEMIES

The Lord is merciful and gracious,
slow to anger and abounding in steadfast love.
He will not always chide,
nor will he keep his anger for ever.
He does not deal with us according to our sins,
nor requite us according to our iniquities.
For as the heavens are high above the earth,
so great is his steadfast love toward those who fear him;
as far as the east is from the west,
so far does he remove our transgressions from us.

PSALM 103:8-12

The best way to know what is central to anyone's beliefs is to listen to what he or she sings. We choose as our favorite songs those which best express the deeper commitments of our lives. This is certainly true today and it was true in ancient Israel. So we find the songs they preserved in the Book of the Psalms, and it is in those songs that we must come most in touch with the basics of their faith.

It quickly becomes clear, then, that fundamental to their understanding of God was their awareness of His love and mercy. Expressed in many ways, this assurance of God's love is the golden thread that runs throughout the psalms. This would be easy to understand if all or most of their experiences had been good. In times of prosperity and peace it is always easy to believe that God loves us. What makes this aspect of Israel's faith so surprising is that their historical experiences had not been basically beneficent. To the contrary, they looked back to slavery in Egypt for the origin of their nation. And for the origin of their kingdom, they looked back to a time of oppression and apostasy in the period of the judges. Instead of great days of national glory, they viewed evil kings, social injustice, military oppression, and periods of being either exiles or fugitives. Yet, throughout all of this they became increasingly convinced of God's love for them and His mercy to them. Now that is incredible!

Their basis for this faith was the conviction that their times of difficulty were God's judgments aimed at turning them from their sin and rebellion. In plain words, He cared *how* they lived. And if He cared how they lived, then He cared for them.

Thus, it was through these times of historical crises that they discovered that God was more concerned with defeating their sin than their enemies. Sin was revealed to be the basic enemy of national and personal life. Thus it was that the psalmist could sing with utmost assurance that out of God's love and mercy, the ultimate enemy would be defeated. But that enemy was within their hearts, not outside. The basic hope of Israel's faith was neither the defeat of Assyria nor the defeat of Babylon, but the defeat of sin. This is the basis of our faith as well. We find in Christ the assurance that our ultimate enemy—sin—will be defeated by God's love and mercy. God's mercy is all-conquering.

O Thou who hast called us to follow Thee, we thank Thee that in following Thee we find forgiveness, mercy, and restoration. In Thy forgiveness we rejoice, and in Thy restoration we live. This we pray through Jesus our Lord. Amen.

chapter sixteen

The Prayer That Communicates

INTERCEDING FOR THE GUILTY

O Lord God, forgive, I beseech thee!
How can Jacob stand? He is so small!

AMOS 7:2

Few Christians would doubt that God speaks words of condemnation and judgment upon sin. Mention the very idea and our minds sweep automatically over the thundering words of prophets such as Amos, Isaiah, Nathan, and Elijah.

Nor would any Christian doubt that God forgives sin. Our minds immediately go to Calvary, where Jesus suffered to bring forgiveness to sinful humanity.

But it is strange that our minds turn to the prophets when we think of judgment and to Jesus when we think of forgiveness. For Jesus surely spoke some words of thundering condemnation. And the prophets are frequently seen as seeking to lead their people into God's forgiveness.

Our text shows us an unexpected picture of God's prophet, Amos. His name is probably associated more with thundering pronouncements of judgment than any other Biblical figure. Yet we find him pleading with God for forgiveness of his people. God's great prophet of judgment was interceding for the guilty!

This is precisely what is so startling! Amos in no way implied that his people were innocent or worthy of forgiveness. He simply begged for two things. First, that God would stop His works of judgment; and second, that He would forgive the guilty. The prophet's only plea was that his people were small, weak, insignificant.

Furthermore, Amos in no way implied that if Israel should be forgiven, they would become loyal, faithful servants of God. He simply rested his plea upon the very nature of the God he served. There is no other basis.

It is sad when we intercede for people simply because it would be good for us to have them as members of our church. It is ridiculous when we intercede for people because they would be significant servants of the kingdom. Who is significant in God's kingdom anyway?

Intercession—real intercession—is based simply on need. Here is someone who needs God's forgiveness. There is a woman who needs God's love. Yonder is a man who needs God's restoration.

For Amos, the real nature of a prophet was not merely speaking to the people on behalf of his God, it was also speaking to God on behalf of his people. He placed himself on the line for his people. This was the measure of his love. But it was also the measure of his understanding of God's love.

It is not enough to condemn sin. The Christian must also intercede for the guilty. We can do no more. We dare do no less.

May we who have been forgiven never forget to intercede for the unforgiven, O Lord. Help us to be more eager to intercede than to condemn, more eager to lead people into Thy presence than to gloat over their coming judgment. Teach us to offer ourselves for the sins of others, even as Thou hast given Thyself for our sins. In Jesus' name we pray. Amen.

REVEALING THE INNER PERSON

And he prayed to the Lord and said, "I pray thee, Lord, is not this what I said when I was yet in my country? That is why I made haste to flee to Tarshish; for I knew that thou art a gracious God and merciful, slow to anger, and abounding in steadfast love, and repentest of evil. Therefore now, O Lord, take my life from me, I beseech thee, for it is better for me to die than to live."

JONAH 4:2-3

Prayer is a mirror in which we can see ourselves if we take the time to look. Far too frequently, we do not even think about our prayers, much less listen to them to hear what we have really said. Let us consider, briefly, this prayer of Jonah. While it was addressed to God, it reveals the inner spiritual nature of this prophet.

Jonah begins by saying to God, "I told you so!" That is a bit arrogant for anyone who is speaking with God. Beyond this, however, it also reveals Jonah's attitude toward the people of Nineveh. God loved them, but Jonah did not. He knew God's merciful nature, and he did not want those hated Assyrians to experience it. However, before we self-righteously condemn him for that, we must at least see that Jonah was honest in his prayer. He did not pretend to have a concern that he did not really feel. Are you and I not guilty at this point? How long has it been since you prayed for the lost somewhere (anywhere) in the world, but were not really concerned enough to do anything about your prayer? Such a prayer reveals that you do not really care either!

Jonah's prayer also reveals the nature of His God. Jonah knew what God was really like. But, having experienced God's love and mercy, he was content with that. This shows that Jonah's experience of God was quite superficial! He had not experienced enough of God's mercy for him to become merciful himself. God was merciful, but Jonah wanted vengeance on his enemies. Jonah did not really care for the Assyrians. Our prayers show much the same thing. We seldom really pray for our enemies. When we do, it is more superficial than real.

Finally, Jonah's prayer revealed his pride. He had announced judgment, but it had not come. Jonah could not stand the humiliation of being wrong. His pride in being right was more important to him than the lives of those multitudes in Nineveh. How often our prayers also reveal our pride-filled natures. Our concerns seem to rest more with our own achievements than with God's grace and mercy.

Prayer is dangerous. We have long known of its danger because of what God can do with it. But we must face the fact that one of its greatest dangers is that it allows God to show us in a spiritual mirror what we are really like. That is a real danger, if you do not want to see yourself. But prayer is also an opportunity for God to begin to change us by first forcing us to see ourselves as we are.

O Thou God of mercy, we thank Thee that in Thy mercy Thou dost show us what we are really like. Use our prayers not only as an avenue to Thy grace and power, but as a means for helping us to become the real servants we can be. This we pray in the name of Jesus. Amen.

PRAYING FROM THE DEPTHS OF LOVE

But, now, if thou wilt forgive their sin
—and if not, blot me, I pray thee,
out of thy book which thou hast written.

EXODUS 32:32

In general, most of our prayers come from the very surface of our hearts and minds. They are usually quickly uttered and just as quickly forgotten. We do not often pause long enough to probe deeply enough within our own beings before we begin to speak to God. In a very real sense, many of our prayers are like water scooped from the surface of the sea—frothy.

Occasionally, we may pause long enough to delve more deeply into our innermost beings before we begin to pray. Then we may bring forth real treasures from the depths of our souls. Here is where we begin to find the real heartbeat of our spirits. Such a prayer was that spoken by Moses and from which we have drawn our text.

Moses was here interceding for his people after their sin of worshipping the golden calf. On many occasions prior to this we have seen Moses intercede for the people. But the intercessory prayer in our text is of a far richer quality. Pleading for God to forgive His rebellious people, Moses went beyond the normal boundaries, expressing his overwhelming love for his people.

Now Moses' prayer was not an expression of an indifferent attitude toward their sin. This is the same Moses who broke the tablets of the Law, confronted his people fearlessly about their sin, demanded quick and immediate decisions, and forced punishment on them. No, he did not take their sin lightly.

But he did take his love for them seriously. He placed his own relationship with God on the line. For good or ill, Moses was going to stand with his people. He stood against their sin, but he loved them just the same. That is real love.

It is quite easy to pray for the lost. It is easy to pray for the lost whom you love because of family relationships. But it is not nearly as easy to place yourself on the line for them when you intercede. That, however, is precisely what Moses did. It is well to note that this is also what Jesus did.

No one would question that we Christians have a mission of intercessory prayer. The question is, however, how do we fulfill it? Do we just pray from the froth of an overflowing love? Or do we probe more deeply into our being and intercede from our innermost depths? It is from such prayers that we are able to express the essence of real, full, overflowing love.

God of grace and mercy, Thou hast called us to intercede for those who do not know Thee. Help us that we may truly be willing to intercede not only with our lips, but with our lives as well. This we pray through the name of Him who so interceded for us. Amen.

> Then Gideon said to God, "If thou wilt deliver Israel by my hand as
> thou hast said, behold, I am laying a fleece of wool on the thresh-
> ing floor; if there is dew on the fleece alone, and it is dry on all the
> ground, then I shall know that thou wilt deliver Israel by my hand,
> as thou hast said."
>
> JUDGES 6:36-37

"I am putting out a fleece." With that statement, many of us have loudly and proudly proclaimed that we are seeking to discover God's will for our lives. Obviously, the quote refers to Gideon's experience.

But take a second look at that statement. Was Gideon really trying to discover God's will for his life? In all honesty, we must answer "No."

Gideon already knew what God wanted him to do. We are told that fact earlier in the account. Furthermore, Gideon actually said as much in our text. He acknowledged that he knew what God wanted him to do by saying, "As thou hast said." Gideon had no question as to what God's purpose for him was.

But this forces us to consider why he went through all the rigamarole with the fleece. Furthermore, when he had his terms met once, why did he repeat the process? At the very best, what Gideon was asking for was additional assurance. Now that is quite human, but it doesn't demand much faith to act after you have been given a miracle. It requires even less when the miracle has been repeated in reverse. If Gideon were seeking more assurance, we could understand his humanity. But he does not stand out as a great man of faith.

On the other hand, there is another possible explanation for Gideon's request. He knew what God wanted him to do, but he may not have wanted to do it. By posing such an impossible sign, he may have been trying to get out of the entire mission. Knowing what God wanted him to do, he may have been simply trying to avoid obeying God's will. Then, when the first demand was met,

Gideon changed the rules, asking for the reverse. This makes me think that Gideon was trying to avoid a difficult task.

The experience of Gideon shows just how easy it is for us to use a spiritual act to try to avoid doing the will of God. Prayer is quite important for the Christian. But it can become a dodge to avoid obedience. Samuel told Saul that "to obey is better than sacrifice" (see 1 Sam. 15:22). To the ancients, sacrifice was a means of communicating with God. It was, in essence, a form of prayer. We are not doing an injustice to the intent of the passage by paraphrasing it to read, "to obey is better than prayer." Let us never become so hypocritical that we substitute prayer for obedience. To pretend to be communicating with God when what we are really seeking to do is to avoid obedient service is the greatest of hypocrisy.

Heavenly Father, forgive us for trying to cover our disobedience with other spiritual exercises. Help us to learn to pray and obey, even as Thy Son did, through whose name we pray. Amen.

CHOOSING THE GOOD WAY

Give thy servant therefore an understanding mind to govern thy people, that I may discern between good and evil; for who is able to govern this thy great people.

1 KINGS 3:9

The ultimate issues of life are quite few in number. We have a tendency to overcomplicate things, but when we get down to the basic issues that make a difference between success and failure, there are really very few.

In the passage leading up to our text, Solomon was met by God and told that he could ask for anything he wanted. What would you have done in similar circumstances? We normally make our prayers to God, piling up long lists of things we want. Solomon was here offered a real opportunity to do what children dream about in fairy tales. But this was no fairy tale. It was the real thing!

If you could have any one thing from God, what would it be? Solomon simply asked for the ability to see the difference between good and evil. What a request that was! Ponder it for a minute.

Think how many heartaches you could have avoided, if you had been able to discern between good and evil.

Think how much joy you could have experienced, if you had known that difference.

Think how much guilt you would have never borne, if you had known that difference.

Think how many failures you would never have faced, if you had known that difference.

Think how many times you would not have had to say "I'm sorry," if you had known that difference.

Think about it.

Now, then, think about something else. Could it be that you and I could have that knowledge if we really asked for it? Could it be that we have so cluttered up our prayers with long lists of "wants" when a simpler, shorter list would have communicated better?

Now in all honesty, we must admit that Solomon had many problems in his life. He had problems within his family, and he also had problems with his government. But he had his problems because he did not *do* the right thing, not because he did not know it.

That is simple.

But it isn't so easy.

O Lord, who hast created the universe and all that is in it, fill us this day anew with the knowledge of the presence of Thy Spirit, *that we may be able both to discern the difference between good and evil and, once having discerned it, to do the good. This we pray in Jesus' name. Amen.*

MAKING ME ACCEPTABLE

Let the words of my mouth
and the meditation of my heart be acceptable
in thy sight, O Lord, my rock and my redeemer.

PSALM 19:14

One of the popular catchwords of contemporary psychology is "self-image."

He has a poor self-image.
She has a healthy self-image.
Joe has an inadequate self-image.
Helen is burdened with a weak self-image.

Perhaps, however, in all these statements our focus is wrong. We get very concerned with our self-image, but how is our "God-image"? How are we seen by God?

The psalmist was not concerned with his self-image. But he was concerned with how God saw him. Could it be that if we are confident about the way God sees us, that we do not have to worry about our self-image? I think that this is true.

The psalmist asked for two things in this prayer. First, he wanted his words to be acceptable to God. Think about that for a moment. How many words have you spoken in the last twenty-four hours that were acceptable to God? Or have you been filling your conversation with other things? This doesn't mean that everything you say must be religious. But it does mean that you should speak only the truth. It also means that you haven't been poking fun at or ridiculing anyone. And it also means that you haven't been gossiping. Have your words been kind or insulting? Have they been gentle or harsh? Have you spoken in the heat of passion and lost control of your words? Have your words been acceptable to God?

The psalmist asked for a second thing as he contemplated his God-image. He asked that the meditations of his heart should also be acceptable to God. That is an even deeper issue. No one else knows what you think. But God does. Have your thoughts of the last twenty-four hours been acceptable to God?

In the Sermon on the Mount (Matt. 5-7), Jesus pointed out that the real problems people have with obedience stem from the thoughts of the heart, before they become the actions of the body. This is still true.

As Christians, our primary problem is not our self-image but our God-image. We need to be more concerned with how God sees us rather than how we see ourselves. But I cannot accomplish this for myself. The only way I can be acceptable to God is if God makes me acceptable. It is for that reason that the psalmist concluded his prayer with the acknowledgment that, for his prayer to be answered, God must be both his Rock and his Redeemer. This is still true today. We must let Him become the Redeemer of our life, the Rock upon which we are established. This must be our prayer.

Almighty God, our Redeemer and our Rock, make us acceptable to Thee, that we may lead others into Thy presence. For Christ's sake we pray. Amen.

---

chapter seventeen

The Compassion That Responds

ACTING TO EXPRESS CONCERN

> Do you think you are a king because you
> compete in cedar? Did not your father eat and drink
> and do justice and righteousness?
> Then it was well with him. He judged the cause
> of the poor and needy; then it was well.
> Is not this to know me? says the Lord.
>
> *JEREMIAH 22:15-16*

It is easy to voice a concern for the problems and burdens that others are forced to bear. We Christians have frequently been accused of doing just that. We voice a concern for the starving masses of the world and for the oppressed inhabitants of the inner cities of our nation. Yet, we stand accused and are frequently guilty of doing absolutely nothing to alleviate these problems.

The question arises, then, and it is a legitimate one, are we really concerned? Do we really care for those whose lives are twisted by oppressive needs.

Jeremiah was attacking just that kind of problem. King Jehoiakim of Judah had sought to show his greatness by building a larger palace than that of his predecessors and by making it more luxurious. The prophet pointed out to him the example of his father, King Josiah, who was acknowledged as a great king. Josiah had gone about the business of being king, doing justice and righteousness. He was not merely content to talk about it, he performed acts that were both good and fair. And lest there be any misunderstanding about what he was talking about, Jeremiah pointed out that Josiah had taken particular steps to be active in seeing that the downtrodden got a fair deal from society. The government stepped in to insure that they were dealt with fairly. The king had expressed his concern for the plight of those helpless citizens through concrete action on their behalf.

Such actions on the part of the king did three things. First, they were good for the king. Somehow, doing good for others always helps those who do it. That should never be the motive, but the results are there nonetheless. Second, doing good for others is good for the nation. When the down-and-out of society are treated well, the whole society prospers. Everyone is better off. Third, doing good for others is a visible manifestation of our relationship with God. The verb *to know* in the Old Testament always reflects personal experience. When we show our concern for others in visible action, we show our relationship with God.

Thus God calls us to express our concern for the needy of the world through specific action. By so doing, we have shown the real nature of our faith and commitment. Words without deeds have no meaning. It is that simple.

Dear God, help us who have been loved by Thee through the life and death of Thy Son to show our love for Thee in our acts of justice, righteousness, and mercy for others. This we pray for the sake of Thy Son, our Lord. Amen.

CELEBRATING WITHOUT CARING

Woe to those who lie upon beds of ivory,
and stretch themselves upon
their couches, and eat lambs from the flock,
and calves from the midst of the stall;
who sing idle songs to the sound of the harp,

and like David invent for themselves
instruments of music; who drink wine in bowls,
and anoint themselves with the finest oils, but are not
grieved over the ruin of Joseph!

AMOS 6:4-6

One of the current words in contemporary churches is *celebration.* We call worship services "celebrations." We call a wedding a "celebration of marriage." We have even called funerals a "celebration of home-going." We call church socials "celebrations of fellowship." The term itself may be very good, but it is in danger of becoming wholly meaningless when it is used for such a variety of experiences.

By itself, the word *celebration* is neither good nor bad. It is how we use it and with what meanings that determine what its real character is.

Consider, for example, the situation Amos described, which was going on in Samaria, the capital of Israel. The whole portrait is one of luxurious celebration. The leading citizens of Samaria were celebrating their prosperity. In fact, if you had asked them, they would surely have declared that they were celebrating the gracious gifts of God. To them, their wealth was an obvious sign of God's blessings.

God was not absent from their minds in their celebrations. The eating of lambs and calves certainly involved worship. In those ancient times, no meat was eaten that had not been properly killed with at least the blood having been offered to God. Furthermore, the songs they sang would probably have been songs of exuberant faith. The comparison with David was certainly one they made themselves.

So the celebrations of those days were directed to God. Of that we can rest fairly well assured. Yet, one thing was missing. God was not in their celebrations, for the luxuriating wealthy were celebrating with no thought for the plight of the "ruin of Joseph." (Joseph is a figure of speech for the entire northern kingdom, since the two largest tribes were descended from Joseph.) The plight of the poor in Amos' day was one of abject poverty accompanied by injustice from the courts and oppression from the wealthy.

Sadly, those celebrations were utterly meaningless. It is one thing to celebrate God's love and mercy. But it is obscene to celebrate God's goodness at the expense of someone else. God is not in such celebrations, nor does He accept them.

Now, what about our celebrations? Are they any less empty? Are we guilty of celebrating God while ignoring those whom God loves? Such celebrations become not worship but blasphemy. Any celebration that is addressed to God and that does not express compassion and concern for the oppressed and downtrodden is a basis for our condemnation, not for our blessing. The woe of the prophet will fall upon the heads of those who pursue such empty celebrations. On that we can rely.

That Thou carest for all Thy people, O Lord, we cannot doubt. Help us who have known Thy love to love others as Thou dost, through Jesus' name we pray. Amen.

RESPONDING TO GOD'S LOVE

Therefore, behold, I will allure her,
and bring her into the wilderness, and speak
tenderly to her.
And there I will give her her vineyards,
and make the Valley of Achor
a door of hope.
And there she shall answer as in the days
of her youth, and as the time
when she came out of the land of Egypt.

HOSEA 2:14-15

Rebellion against God is frequently described in terms of marital infidelity. Here Hosea turned the image around and described

God's redemptive compassion in terms of a brokenhearted Husband who sought to win back the love of His unfaithful wife.

To fully grasp the impact of our text, there are several images we must understand. First, one of the bases of Israel's infidelity to God rested in a false understanding of God's nature. Israel knew that God was a God of victorious deliverance, for He had brought them out of Egypt. But when they arrived in Canaan, they wondered whether or not their God could really grow crops. The Baals (false gods) of Canaan had been producing crops for the Canaanites, or so they thought, for generations. So Israel turned to the Canaanite Baals for fruitfulness and to the God of Israel when they needed deliverance. Hosea's announcement was that God was going to take them back into the wilderness and show them that He could produce vineyards there. Any god could grow grapes in Canaan, but only the God of Israel could grow grapes in the wilderness!

The second image we must grasp concerns the Valley of Achor. This was the place where Achan was executed for his sin at Jericho. It had stood out in Israel's memory as a symbol of disobedience to God, of defeat because of that disobedience, and of despair because of the nature of sin. Yet Hosea announced to his people that not only could God grow grapes wherever He wished, but He could transform the symbol of their sin, rebellion, and defeat into a gateway of hope. That is the nature of God's power and love.

Thus the prophet promised his people that God was going to woo them again, demonstrating both His power and the overabundance of His transforming love. God's love had not been destroyed. That merciful love still reached out to Israel, seeking to win her back to her commitment to Him.

The ultimate end of Hosea's proclamation was that God's love was going to win out. Israel would respond; she would answer to God when He called her, coming to Him in loving obedience, turning her back on her infidelities.

That is our hope also. God's love for us does not end when we sin. He loves us still. So He calls us, enabling us to turn back to

Him with our own loving response. The image is one of tenderness, compassion, and strength. God's love will conquer. When we have forsaken Him, He will not leave us alone. On that we can rely.

O Thou great God of love, help us begin to comprehend the greatness of Thy love, that we may respond to Thy love in obedience and faithfulness. This we pray in the name of Him who showed us Thy love most fully, even Jesus, our Lord. Amen.

WELCOMING THE OUTCAST

But Esau ran to meet him, and embraced him, and fell on his neck and kissed him, and they wept. . . . Jacob said, "No, I pray you, if I have found favor in your sight, then accept my present from my hand; for truly to see your face is like seeing the face of God, with such favor have you received me."

GENESIS 33:4, 10

Did you ever get your life in such a mess that you thought there was no place to turn? At such times it appears that every way we turn leads to a worse situation, and there is just no way out of our troubles.

Jacob was in such a situation. He had been forced to flee from his own home because of his fear of the vengeance of Esau. After spending twenty years as an exile with his Uncle Laban, Jacob had once again been forced to flee because of the anger of Laban and his sons.

This left Jacob with no place to go. There were an angry uncle and cousins behind him and a vengeful brother in front of him. Then he was brought the frightening news that Esau was coming to meet him with four hundred men. At that moment, everything caved in on Jacob.

If that weren't enough, Jacob had spent the night wrestling

with the angel of the Lord. During the night, he had made his peace with God, finding forgiveness, restoration, and a new nature. That at least brought him spiritual peace. But it did not change his external situation. He was still threatened by angry men on every side.

Suddenly Jacob was confronted by Esau. Yet nothing happened as he had feared and expected. Instead of meeting him with hostility and wrath, Esau greeted Jacob with love, welcoming him home. Jacob recognized that such a response was precisely like the experience he had had with God the morning before.

When Jacob looked at Esau, he was reminded of God. Now, there was little that was attractive about Esau. He was a rough outdoorsman, with a weather-beaten face, a very hairy man who seldom bathed, as he is described as smelling like a goat. Yet Jacob looked at Esau and thought of God. It was not the physical but spiritual resemblance that caught Jacob's eye. Esau greeted his brother—the one he had every reason to despise—with open arms of love. He welcomed the one who had done him wrong with abundant forgiveness. It was this that reminded Jacob of God, for this is precisely the way God is and what God does.

The Biblical image of God is always of One who welcomes home the outcast rebel. He sees the rootlessness, the hopelessness, the guilt, and the despair in us. Even though we frequently do not turn to Him until we have exhausted all our resources, yet God's loving mercy is still there. We should never presume on God's mercy. But the amazing truth of the Biblical portrait of our Lord is that He waits for us with patient love, welcoming us into His abundance. This is a compassion that responds to our need. How wonderful!

Dear God, we cannot understand why Thou dost love us when we are rebels, or how Thou canst love us who have been disloyal. But we rejoice in Thy assurance that Thy compassions fail not. In that compassion we bask, knowing that Thy love is truly sufficient for all our needs. Through Jesus Christ we pray. Amen.

Then Saul said, "I have done wrong; return, my son David, for I will no more do you harm, because my life was precious in your eyes this day; behold, I have played the fool, and have erred exceedingly."

1 SAMUEL 26:21

One of the more tragic statements of all times is this: "I have played the fool." How often, when we look back on some situation through which we have just gone, can we say these words? In the cast of characters for a play, there is nothing wrong with having had the part of the fool. But in real life, there is not one of us who really wants to be a fool.

Yet we do play the fool. We are foolish to ignore the demands of God on our lives. We are foolish to ignore the pain and anguish in those round about us. We who are wise enough not to play with fire are foolish enough to play with war and nuclear arms. We are foolish enough to think that we can play around with sin and rebellion and not have to face the consequences. Truly, we do play the fool.

In Saul's situation, he had been jealous over David and had sought to destroy the young man who had meant so much to his kingdom. Jealousy had blinded him, turning into rage and anger. Instead of spending his time being a good king, Saul had played the fool and turned his entire attention to the extermination of one man. Yet, when David had held the life of Saul in his hand, he had mercifully spared the king. He had loved the one who hated him, and spared the one who sought to kill him. That is mercy and compassion in abundant measure.

The mercy and compassion of David struck a responsive chord in the heart of Saul. They forced the great king, so proud in his might, into an admission of guilt. David's love caused Saul to identify his own sin. But Saul did more than recognize his own sin, he confessed it to David, admitting his own folly. At least, Saul at this point did not try to blame his errors on his advisors. He accepted the guilt as his own, admitting his folly.

The love of God, expressed toward us in compassion and mercy, should lead us to something of a similar experience. It is God's love that really causes us to see our own sinfulness. But His love and mercy should lead us beyond merely recognizing our sins; they should also lead us to confessing our sins. It is never easy to admit that we are sinners. It is even less easy to admit that we have acted foolishly. But we must make this difficult admission in response to God's compassion if we are to experience the full benefit of that compassion. For God's compassionate mercy only cleanses sin when we have confessed it. It is through our admission of folly and sin that we finally find forgiveness.

The first step to real wisdom, then, is the admission, "I have played the fool." It is not an easy admission, but it is a necessary one. Then God forgives us for our folly.

Merciful and compassionate God, grant to us the awareness of our own sin and foolishness. Keep us from trying to blame others for our failures. Help us to confess our folly, that we may find forgiveness and mercy through Thy grace. Help us to become forgiving of others' folly even as Thou hast forgiven ours. Through Jesus' holy name we pray. Amen.

DECIDING TO ACT

When I heard these words I sat down and wept, and mourned for days; and I continued fasting and praying before the God of heaven. . . . And I said to the king, "If it pleases the king, and if your servant has found favor in your sight, that you send me to Judah, to the city of my fathers' sepulchres, that I may rebuild it."

NEHEMIAH 1:4; 2:5

It may sometimes seem that Christians believe that all compassion comes from God. The Bible is quick to reveal what experience also readily shows, that humans are frequently compassionate as well.

Now that should not be surprising, for we are made in the image of God, and God is compassionate. But let us never get the idea that God has a corner on compassion or even that Christians do. That is just not so. He did not make us that way.

However, there is a dimension to both divine and human compassion that we need to consider more closely. We generally speak and think in such a way as to indicate that compassion is primarily an emotion. That is quite false. In the Biblical message, compassion is always active. It responds with feeling to someone's need. But it also responds with action.

Nehemiah was a Hebrew who had risen to a position of prominence and confidence in the court of the king of Persia. When he learned of the devastation of his homeland and of the destitute condition of his people, his emotions were stirred. He immediately followed a very natural path for a person of deep religious faith; he began to pray about it. He discovered through his prayer that God was also concerned about the plight of Judah. Nehemiah also discovered that God was going to use him to help meet Judah's desperate need. We may frequently find that when our compassion is stirred enough to get us praying about any specific need, that we may be the instrument chosen to meet that need.

Thus Nehemiah was led to do more about Judah's tragic situation than pray about it, he took the first step toward meeting that need by asking his king for permission to go and do something for the people of Judah. Genuine compassion is always more than merely getting disturbed about a situation. It does lead us to act to meet that need.

For the Christian, the first act is usually the act of prayer. But it should seldom end there. When all we do about any crisis is pray about it, we are seldom doing enough. God himself is an active God. His compassion led Him into His great redemptive act for all people. We, who follow Him, must be led to act in similar ways. If our compassion is not active, it is not really compassion.

Such acts may lead us to put our lives on the line. It may be dangerous and frequently risky. But consider what God's compassion cost Him. Consider what Jesus' compassion cost Him. Is there any doubt that real compassion is—and must be—costly? If there is a need that grips your heart or stirs your imagination, let your compassion lead you to put yourself on the line to meet that need. That is the path of redemptive action.

O Thou who hast loved us for all time and hast showed Thy love through the life and death of Jesus Christ, help us who follow Thee to show our love for others by our lives and, if need be, by our deaths. This we pray in Jesus' name. Amen.

chapter eighteen

The Joy That Celebrates

CELEBRATING IN THE FACE OF DEFEAT

> Though the fig tree do not blossom,
> nor fruit be on the vines,
> the produce of the olive fail
> and the fields yield no food,
> the flock be cut off from the fold
> and there be no herd in the stalls,
> yet I will rejoice in the Lord,
> I will joy in the God of my salvation.
>
> *HABAKKUK 3:17-18*

Celebration! As we have noted, that word is much in our vocabulary today. Christians speak of worship as celebration. Many people describe parties as celebrations. Frequently, life itself is called a celebration. Even the defeat of an enemy can be termed a celebration, or at least it becomes the basis of a celebration.

Obviously, a term so widely used and in such varied contexts is in danger of losing its meaning. Perhaps we ought to ask, then, what is the real meaning of celebration? Whatever else may be included, a celebration is a time of rejoicing. Now it seems to me that this is precisely what Habakkuk was talking about. His attention was focused on his celebration before God.

But look at the life situation that surrounded the prophet's celebration. He was living in a time when everything that could go wrong had apparently done so. He was considering a time of utter defeat and destitution. His crops had failed, his flocks had been destroyed, and everything in his life was coming up thorns and thistles.

Yet, against such a background, the prophet found the faith and courage to celebrate before God. Now this does not mean that he was celebrating his destitution. What it does reflect is his sense that God was more important to him than any of the "things" of life. The prophet did not reveal the reasons for this assurance, merely his commitment to it. To him, God's presence was a basis for celebration, for rejoicing.

This should be true for us as well.

It is so sad when someone who has been a faithful servant of God when times were good turns away from Him when times are bad. Yet this frequently happens. The testimony of God's great saints has been that they found their greatest comfort and support from God in the bad times. This can be true for us, and it should be.

You and I need to examine our relationship with God, to determine if it is merely a "good times" faith. If our trust in God cannot sustain us when everything comes loose, it is not all that it should be.

We need, then, to discover the real nature of a faith commitment to God. We must discover what His sustaining love can do for us in all of life's circumstances. Sorrows and tragedies will come. They are a part of life. We need a faith that can celebrate the presence of God even when the bad times come. This is the faith that will sustain. Anything less is too little.

Merciful God, help us to learn to rejoice in Thy presence, even when our life conditions seem to leave us little to celebrate. May we find in Thee strength for the weakness that overcomes us, peace for the conflict that terrorizes us, and love for our aloneness. In Jesus' name we pray. Amen.

Rejoice greatly, O daughter of Zion!
Shout aloud, O daughter of Jerusalem!
Lo, your king comes to you; triumphant and victorious
is he, humble and riding
on an ass, on a colt the foal of an ass.

ZECHARIAH 9:9

When life caves in on you and everything goes wrong, when loved ones have proven either mortal or unfaithful, when trusted friends have been unreliable, is there anything to help you keep going? The answer to that question is simply, "It depends." Sometimes in such a situation, a deep depression sets in that makes some people suicidal. They simply decide that life is not worth living. For others, the depression sets in too, but the fear of pain and death keeps them from following such an extreme measure. Still others exist in a state of shock, not really comprehending the real situation that has overtaken them.

But there are those who, while deeply feeling the pressures that have come, manage to keep on living. They start putting the pieces of life together again, getting on with the business of living. What is it that enables them to face the darkness without surrendering to it? While there are certainly many answers to this, and not one of them is simple, there is an obvious answer we need to consider. The main thing that keeps us going in days of darkness and despair is hope.

Now the hope of which I speak is not just an unrealistic idealism, nor is it a visionary dream with no basis. The only hope that will sustain us in the pit of deepest despair is a hope that has been proven through the passage of time, a hope that is based on an authority we have already found to be reliable.

For the nation of Judah, it appeared that all history had turned against them. Yet the hope of a future king who would reign over them in meekness and in victory was able to sustain them. It offered sustenance to them because they had experienced

God's deliverances in the past. They could therefore trust Him to keep His promises for the future.

We who live on this side of the Cross know how God fulfilled that hope in Jesus. He came as the conquering King—conquering sin and self—and entered their experience with gentle meekness. He did not challenge Rome on a white charger. He showed that His claim to kingship was over the hearts of men, ruling from within. Yet, we also know that this was not the end of the story. We now look forward to the coming time when Christ shall rule over all the kingdoms of men. He will still be meek and gentle, but He will also be the future King of this universe. This is our hope.

Whatever life brings to us, we have hope in Christ. He has saved us and will keep us with Himself. Ultimately, He will rule on this earth. Even when the world has done its worst, it is never the end of the story. It is quite true that Christ Jesus brings faith to our hearts and love to our lives. But He also sustains us through hope. Therefore, we can rejoice in Him, no matter what comes. Life with Christ now is good. But life with Christ in the future will assuredly be better. No matter what comes, the story has not ended yet.

Merciful God, help us to find a basis for rejoicing in the hope Jesus brings. This we pray in His precious name. Amen.

SINGING IN VICTORY

And Miriam sang to them: "Sing to the Lord, for he has triumphed gloriously; the horse and the rider he has thrown into the sea."

EXODUS 15:21

When the human heart feels deeply, it sings. You and I find music to express the deepest emotions of our lives. Even when we do not sing ourselves, we regularly turn to music of some sort to express those things we feel which are too deep for words.

If you wish to discover what a certain church really believes—not just its "official" doctrine, but its real life commitments—listen to the songs that are regularly sung. If you want to know just what your community's basic commitments are, listen to the "Top Forty" radio show, where the most popular music of the day is sung. It will express the hopes and fears, the dreams and goals of that particular moment.

Our text reflects such an insight. The people of Israel had just been brought out of Egypt. Pinned against the sea, by the pursuing army of Egypt, they had given up hope. Yet, at that moment, they had experienced a miraculous deliverance. It matters little how it occurred. The thing is that they were delivered precisely when they needed to be. Safely on the other side of the sea, they burst into a song of celebration, rejoicing in the victory God had won for them.

Let us not be guilty of judging those ancient peoples by the morality of a Christian era. In our more sober moments, we decry the celebration of the defeat and destruction of an enemy. But, at the moment of deliverance, there is always a sense of celebration. When life has been spared, we do wish to sing and dance. The heart does rejoice when a seemingly hopeless situation has been transformed into a victory.

So we should not condemn them for celebrating the defeat of a foe. That was not what they were really celebrating. They were celebrating God's deliverance. They had stared death in the face and had been delivered. This is their reason for rejoicing.

Let us then join in their celebration. When we who have such difficulty holding on to hope, find that hope vindicated, it is worth celebrating. But let us note that their celebration was directed toward God. It was He who had saved them. They were not responsible.

The same should be true of our victory celebrations. It is always God who gives the victory. He must be the object of our celebration and the recipient of our praise. We may even be able to identify a more immediate cause of our victory. But the ultimate cause is always God.

Furthermore, His final, ultimate victory for us is the victory over sin. He delivers us from that which enslaves and oppresses us, and removes our guilt. That is worthy of celebration. Praise God!

O Thou who hast delivered us in times past from the penalty of sin, and who in Christ Jesus art delivering us from the power of sin, we rejoice in that Thou wilt ultimately deliver us from the very presence of sin. In this we rejoice through Christ Jesus, Thy Son, our Lord. Amen.

GIVING IN ABUNDANCE

Then Araunah said to David, "Let my lord the king take and offer up what seems good to him; here are the oxen for the burnt offering and the threshing sledges and the yokes of the oxen for the wood. All this, O king, Araunah gives to the king." And Araunah said to the king, "The Lord your God accept you." But the king said to Araunah, "No, but I will buy it of you for a price; I will not offer burnt offerings to the Lord my God which cost me nothing."

2 SAMUEL 24:22-24a

It is a sad but tragic fact of Christian life that many of us complain as soon as anyone begins to talk about money. We have long been willing to dedicate almost anything to God but our money.

How different from this attitude is that professed by both of the characters in our scriptural vignette. David, the king, was seeking to obtain both a place and the animals to offer a sacrifice to God. He determined the location and sought to buy the place from the owner, Araunah. This would have provided an easy occasion for the farmer to take advantage of David's desire to worship. Thus he could have named an exorbitant price. Not only did Araunah not do this, rather he sought to honor both the king and his

God by giving the place and the sacrificial victims. He was openly generous and God-honoring with his possessions. There was no reluctance on the part of Araunah.

But David revealed himself in the same light. He could easily have taken advantage of the farmer's generosity, accepting all his gifts and using them to worship his God. By so doing, he would have had a magnificent ceremony of worship that would have cost the king nothing. This would have been quite easy for the king to justify, for he needed all his resources to accomplish those things for God to which he had dedicated himself. Yet David rejected this plan. He would have no part in offering something to God that had cost him nothing.

It is clear, then, that both our heroes were men who desired to celebrate the worship of God by offering gifts that were quite costly. It was not their desire to get by with as little as possible in giving. Rather, they both sought to give the very best they had to God. Nothing else would have satisfied their own need. And nothing else would have honored God.

Those of us who truly wish to celebrate in worship all that God has done for us should not be content with any less either. We should offer to God that which honors Him and that which expresses the deepest gratitude of our heart. We have seen that Jesus gave His life for us. Certainly nothing less than sacrificial giving will offer real praise to Him. We should not be satisfied with anything less. We cannot offer more.

Gracious God, Thou who hast given Thine own Son for us, help us to want to give to Thee offerings that will honor Thee and glorify Thy name in all the earth. Having helped us to want to give, grant to us the determination to give in like manner as Thou hast given to us. This we pray in the name of Jesus Christ. Amen.

ACCEPTING GOD'S ABUNDANCE

Thou preparest a table before me in the presence
of my enemies; thou anointest my head
with oil, my cup overflows.

PSALM 23:5

Anyone who has resources can give generously. It is a far more difficult thing to accept gifts graciously. We who are followers of Christ Jesus have His example of how to give generously, with no thought of repayment. Yet we obviously have a long way to go in order to learn how to truly give as He has given.

But we find the other side of the coin even more difficult. We find it quite hard to accept God's gifts graciously. Let us consider the image that the psalmist has drawn for us.

Here we have the portrait of a generous host setting forth a feast for his friends. Even when the friends are surrounded by enemies, the gracious host sets forth the banquet. At the same time, the host becomes the guard, keeping the enemies at bay.

In the ancient Near East, bathing was done infrequently. Thus when a guest came, the host made the guest acceptable by anointing him with a sweet-smelling ointment. The host was very careful to honor and make his guest feel welcome. But the final image is even more striking.

As a child, when I read this psalm, I could think of nothing more messy than a cup that overflowed on the tablecloth. I got in trouble when I spilled a glass of tea. Imagine the mess you would have with a cup of wine that constantly overflowed red fluid on to a spotless white cloth. In the Hebrew language, however, a different picture is painted from that of our more traditional translation. There is no verb in the last phrase. It actually says, "my cup—abundance." It is not a picture of a glass that constantly overflows. Rather, it is the picture of a very attentive host. Every time I drink a little from my glass, the host refills it again. I never have to wait for something to quench my thirst. There is always an abundant supply in my glass, because the host keeps it full.

That is the picture of God's gracious gifts to you and to me. He never allows us to run dry. He is always at hand, supplying the things we really need for the banquet in His presence. This does not mean that He meets every need we think we have. Rather, He meets our real needs. We may ask for ice cream and receive only bread. But He will never give us stones when we need bread. He meets the real needs of our lives. And He meets those needs abundantly.

This puts the real task, then, upon us. We must learn to accept God's abundant gifts with gratitude. But we must accept them. It is not easy to always be on the receiving end of His generosity. But that is precisely where we are. It is His overabundant love that constantly gives to us. It would be the height of folly to fail to accept His abundance.

O God of gracious giving, help us to accept Thy gifts with a response of love. Grant to us grateful hearts, quick to accept Thy goodness and to rejoice in it. May Thy Spirit help us to live with thanksgiving, through Jesus' name we pray. Amen.

BLESSING THROUGH FORGIVENESS

Blessed is he whose transgression
is forgiven, whose sin is covered.

PSALM 32:1

Of all the reasons for celebrating known to the heart and mind of humankind, I know of no greater one than the fact God forgives sin. God in His infinite mercy literally comes to bury our sin. He covers it so that it cannot be seen, known, or experienced again. It is gone! That is a wonderful reason for celebrating.

But not only does God bury our sin so that it cannot be seen, He also forgives it. Now when God forgives sin, He also forgets it.

It is gone forever. Suddenly, our life, which has been burdened by guilt or warped by impurity, is released. We are at last free to become what God intended us to be.

It is almost as if we were like the lowly caterpillar. He appears to be an ugly creepy-crawler, doomed to be confined to the ground for life or, at best, to the leaves of trees. Then, suddenly, one day he is transformed into a lovely butterfly. Now he is both beautiful and free. He is no longer a prisoner of the earth; he can fly!

So can we, when our sins are forgiven. We are freed from the bonds that tie us to the ugly, sordid sins of our lives. At last, we can become what God intended for us. Furthermore, while becoming, we can celebrate our release and our freedom.

There is one more idea in our text from which we can profit, and that is the word *blessed*. It sounds so sacred, almost as if it were encased in stained glass. When we are classified as "blessed," we feel so sanctimonious. But the Hebrew word translated "blessed" is anything but super pious. It is a concept that might better be translated as, "Oh, how happy," or perhaps as, "Oh, the happiness of." It implies a sort of exuberant effervescence, a kind of joy that is almost giddy, verging on the lightheadedness that accompanies the first stages of drunkenness. This is the kind of joyful exuberance that the apostles and disciples had on the day of Pentecost, when God's Holy Spirit descended on them.

This kind of joyous celebration literally gives us a sense of no longer being earthbound. At last, we are free to fly. When God forgives our sin and buries it in the past, He frees us to fly. Now we can mount up on eagle's wings. We are freed for fellowship with Him. We can enter into His presence with no sense of guilt, for the guilt is gone.

It is this kind of joyous celebration that overflows from the life of anyone who has been forgiven. Those who haven't known God's pardon can only faintly grasp the idea of the joy that overwhelms the forgiven heart. Those of us who have been forgiven have a reason for real celebration. Ours is no counterfeit joy, but the real thing. At last, and forever, we are free!

O Thou God of wondrous joy, we could not grasp the joy of Thy forgiveness until we had been forgiven. Help us to try to share that overwhelming joy through our celebrations, that others may come to experience Thy forgiveness as well. This we pray in the name of Him who made your love visible and your forgiveness real, even Jesus our Lord. Amen.

Index